Soon as the ev'ning fhades prevail,
The Moon takes up her wondrous tale,
And nightly, to the lift'ning Earth,
Repeats the ftory of her birth.
While all the Orbs that round her burn,
And all the Planets in their turn,
Proclaim the tidings, as they roll,
And fpread the truth, from pole to pole.

THE
STARRY RUBRIC

SEVENTEENTH-CENTURY ENGLISH ASTROLOGY AND MAGIC

THE STARRY RUBRIC:
SEVENTEENTH-CENTURY ENGLISH ASTROLOGY AND MAGIC
Copyright © 2012 Alexander Cummins
Published by Hadean Press, France
Hadean Press is an imprint of Circle Six
Cover art 'The Astrologer' by Hans Holbein the Younger, 1538.
Frontispiece taken from *The Book of Knowledge*, by Erra
Pater and made English by William Lilly, published 1794 by
Thomas Spencer in New York.

Printed in Great Britain.

ISBN 978 1 907881 21 3

HADEAN PRESS

www.hadeanpress.com

THE
STARRY RUBRIC

SEVENTEENTH-CENTURY ENGLISH ASTROLOGY AND MAGIC

ALEXANDER CUMMINS

GRATITUDES

THERE ARE A GREAT MANY PEOPLE TO THANK FOR THE existence of this book. Most obviously, I'd like to thank Erze and Dis for putting it out, and for all the effort that such a publishing endeavour entails. I'd also like to thank Jake Stratton-Kent, for introducing Team Hadean and I in the first place and, significantly, for providing both some incredibly useful material for the work and a uniquely savvy and experienced perspective. This book is an expansion of my post-graduate research degree thesis, and as such there are several people without whom it would not exist: most notably, Raphael Hallet, who deserves special recognition for his kindly and expert academic supervision. Over the course of writing the thesis, Noel Heath, Luke Massey, Luke Roberts, and Joy Preece all cast critical proofing eyes over it, for which I am incredibly grateful. I'd also like to thank Phil Dacey for the lively debate.

In expanding thesis into book, I was fortunate enough to have had a great many ears to bend and shoulders to cry on. I would like to thank Ronald Hutton both for his professional academic support and advice, and for his friendship and kindness. Special thanks should also go to Dave Evans, Brian Paisley, Sam Webster, and Amy Hale for their unique perspectives on the history of magic and for their camaraderie. Likewise, I would like to acknowledge fellow post-graduate friends Will Raybould, Pete Evans, Gideon Shapiro, and Margery Masterson for their continuing support. I am also incredibly grateful to Samantha Piggott, Nancy Douglas, Phil Legard, and all of the other eleventh-hour proofreading friends and family.

Any mistakes remaining in this work are the result of my continued tampering and tinkering.

I would also like to personally thank Tamsin MacDonald, Byron Vincent, Raphael Attar, Katie Challis, Jonathan Adam Sidle, Amie Pulfer, Helen Grey, Alis Kay, and James Wheale for all of their compassion, patience and encouragement.

Lastly, and most importantly, I would like to express my gratitude and admiration for my mother Anne, my father Mike, and my sister Harriet. Without their unwavering support and love absolutely none of this would be possible.

Thank you.

Alexander Cummins

ABSTRACT

THIS BOOK EXAMINES THE FUNCTIONS OF ASTROLOGY in early modern England. The history of astrology has, with a few notable exceptions, considered astrology in terms of emerging science, declining magic, or in terms of a "rationality" defined as an essentially non-magical endeavour. This book considers early modern expectations and practical applications of astrology, and models astrology's universal scope using three areas of focus – the environmental, the political and the social. The environmental focus discusses how astrology informed human understanding and action in relation to the nature and passage of time as well as phenomena of the natural world. The political focus examines the astrologer's role as an interpreter of divine ordering, while also underlining the power of astrological knowledge to affect as well as analyse. The social focus analyses astrology's conception of the individual and the forces influencing their predispositions and temperaments. It also addresses the numerous ways in which astrology offered active solutions and remedies for the variety of personal questions, concerns and problems it mapped and interpreted. This book analyses the ways in which magic and astrology co-mingled, cross-pollinated and fused, as well as emphasising the theories and techniques that unified all scales of existence in a grand interrelating astrological system. Finally, this book explores the performative and transformative dimensions of astrological practice, which produced intercessory knowledge and action through an interrelated set of functions, interpretative techniques and ritualised activities.

Contents

CHAPTER 1
INTRODUCTIONS

ASTROLOGY IS AN IMPORTANT AREA OF STUDY IN THE history of seventeenth-century England. It has been described as 'a central – if controversial – feature of the intellectual and social history of the early modern period'.[1] Astrological theory and techniques were used to analyse all manner of phenomena – it has been remarked that astrology was 'less a separate discipline than an aspect of a generally accepted world picture.'[2] This book concerns itself with the multiplicity of specific uses to which astrology was put, including such diverse fields as early modern cosmology, eschatology, political analysis and propaganda, medicine and popular magical solutions to personal problems. In doing so, it advances three contentions.

Firstly, that astrology presented and explored a thoroughly interconnected universe, to the extent that it posited the interdependence of individuals and their environment – meaning both one's immediate surroundings and the wider totality of the universe. Humanity was not considered an agency outside of or separated from the "natural world": *all* phenomena, human and otherwise, were unified in a total and interrelated astrological spectrum of meaning. As demonstrated by the wide variety of subject

---

1   Michael MacDonald, 'The Career of Astrological Medicine in England', in *Religio Medici: Medicine and Religion in Seventeenth-century England,* ed. O.P. Grell and A. Cunningham (Aldershot, 1996), p. 62.

2   Keith Thomas, *Religion and the Decline of Magic* (London, 1991 reprint), p. 338.

matter in the sources I have used, astrology touched on everything. Nothing, save perhaps God Himself, was beyond astrological analysis. The unifying and underlying influences of and on anything could be discerned, analysed and manipulated.

Secondly, this book argues that astrology based this analysis and manipulation of influence on fundamentally magical principles that described the nature and operations of the universe. This nature was understood and manipulated through ontological taxonomies, such as the four classical elements and rulerships of the seven planets. These operations were understood and manipulated through magical axioms, such as reflection, contagion, similitude and the agency of non-material intelligences. As such, magic and astrology intermingled in a mutually supportive exploration, analysis and application of occult theories and practices. To explore this, I will be drawing upon explanations from works of occult philosophy as well as astrological handbooks.

Finally, this book puts forward the notion that astrological knowledge and action were themselves fused and interrelated. Investigative astrological activity produced complex forms of knowledge – divinatory foreknowledge of coming events clearly demonstrates how magical ways of knowing shaped action. The interpretive and intercessional functions that astrological practitioners performed for themselves and their various clients are also considered significant indicators of the power of occult knowledge. Furthermore, the transformative effects of astrological knowledge in and of a magical universe frequently combined and united divination and enchantment activities, and demonstrate more generally that understanding was itself a form of knowledge-in-action. Accounts of the astrological services offered by practitioners are therefore invaluable.

The seventeenth century was a turbulent, uncertain time for England. The political and social turmoil of the Civil War, the Revolution, the Commonwealth and the Restoration Crisis were accompanied by intellectual upheaval: eschatological concerns combining politics, religion and cosmology were among the flood of new and often socially disruptive ideas being discussed and disseminated throughout this period. Fundamental to this rise in new ways to make sense of a changing world was the lifting of printing press censorship and restrictions between 1640 and 1660. These 'several years of virtually complete freedom of the press' were crucial to the spread of new ideas during this century, as this freedom 'offered the possibility of choice between alternatives, [and] ended the state church's monopoly of opinion-forming.'[3] Astrology played an important part in this explosion in publishing – from political analysis in almanacs and pamphlet propaganda to astrological diagnostics, treatments and elaborations on contemporary Galenic humoural theory in popular medical handbooks. There were also strong astrological components within continental grimoires of magic being translated, printed and bought around this period, not to mention the production and sales of 'huge numbers of chapbooks on astrology and divination.'[4] This century marks a zenith in the availability and popularity of astrology and its uses in England.

Studying how early modern thinkers characterised and understood their world is vital in constructing accurate assessments of their experiences. Astrology in seventeenth-century England was used to inform decision-making and

3   Christopher Hill, *Some Intellectual Consequences of the English Revolution* (London, 1980), p. 7, 49.

4   Owen Davies, *Grimoires: A History of Magic Books* (Oxford, 2009), p. 132.

problem-solving, to interpret both personal crises and historical events, and to manage and manipulate diverse activities. It is important to consider astrology because it was important to the early modern people we study.

(A Brief) Historiography

One of the first major works of the twentieth century to deal with the history of astrology was Lynn Thorndike's extensive *A History of Magic and Experimental Science*, published in eight volumes between 1923 to 1958. It located astrology within a grand positivist narrative of the rise of the experimental methodology and the birth of science, spanning from Pliny to the end of the seventeenth century. The series concentrated upon the intellectual, and above all scientific, aspects of astrology and magic. Thorndike assesses that astrology's main role was to be an important precursor for future scientific ideology. This approach demonstrates how the history of astrology (and of magic in general) began the twentieth century by being assessed, not by its own standards and achievements, but by those of science.

Over the 1960s, Harry Rusche emphasised a specific political context to seventeenth-century English astrology with his 1965 article 'Merlini Anglici: Astrology and Propaganda from 1644 to 1651'.[5] His later article, 'Prophecies and Propaganda, 1641 to 1651',[6] underlined links between astrology and magical prophecy by examining interpretive roles of astrologers in forming specific political analyses from the symbolic language of magical prophecy. Magic and astrology were demonstrated to offer an interrelated set of

---

5   *English Historical Review, 80* (1965), p. 322-333.

6   *English Historical Review*, 84 (October, 1969), p. 752-770.

functions for assessing and affecting political developments. The 1966 publication of the diary and correspondences of the magical practitioner, patron and antiquarian Elias Ashmole (1617-1692), edited by C.H. Josten, offered insight into the personal practice and understanding of astrological techniques of a renowned seventeenth-century occultist.[7]

Keith Thomas' *Religion and the Decline of Magic* (London, 1971), regarded as a landmark work in the history of magic, also contained important contributions to the history of astrology. This book treated astrology as a fundamental part of the early modern English understanding of a magical universe. Its "bottom-up" perspective described astrologer's consultation rooms and magical surgery sessions to explore the uses and social significance of astrology. It also marked a fundamental shift in historical considerations of astrological magic, away from demonstrating how science "evolved" from magic and towards assessment of the changes that rendered magic inadequate – or, as G.E.R. Lloyd put it, 'the explanandum is not, in any case, the victory of rationality over magic: there was no such victory; but rather how the criticism of magic got some purchase.'[8] However, perhaps one of the most important contributions to the history of English astrology was the publication of Bernard Capp's *Astrology and the Popular Press: English Almanacs 1500-1800* (London, 1979). This book emphasised the social, intellectual and cultural importance of almanacs and astrology – demonstrating their wide-ranging influences on, *inter alia,* literacy, politics, agriculture, religion, romance, cosmology,

---

7   C.H. Josten (ed.), *Elias Ashmole (1617-1692): his autobiographical and historical notes, his correspondence, and other contemporary sources relating to his life and work* (Oxford, 1966).

8   G.E.R. Lloyd, *Magic, Reason and Experience: Studies in the Origins and Development of Greek Science* (Cambridge, 1979), p. 263-4.

medicine, advertising and history itself. It located a firm astrological contribution to the importance of print in early modern English culture. Astrology was dealt with on its own terms, in its own language, and through the accounts of a whole spectrum of contemporary practitioners, believers and sceptics.

The 1980s saw various refinements in understanding astrology's significance in seventeenth-century England. Stephen Skinner's *Terrestrial Astrology: Divination by Geomancy* (London, 1980) demonstrated how crucial astrological symbolism was for geomantic divination, emphasising ontological interdependencies of early modern magic and astrology. One of the most important works of this decade for the history of astrology was Michael MacDonald's *Mystical Bedlam: Madness, Anxiety and Healing in Seventeenth Century England* (Cambridge, 1981) which emphasised psychiatric contexts within which seventeenth-century English astrology operated. It explored the theories and techniques of astrological medicine, with particular interest in early modern conceptions of "mental health", by focusing on the practice of the clergyman, astrologer and magician Richard Napier (1559-1634), and yielded valuable data from statistical analysis of Napier's detailed casenotes. S.J. Tester's *A History of Western Astrology* (Bury St. Edmunds, 1987) traced astrology as a discrete system back to ancient Greece and up to the late Renaissance, offering an important understanding of the basis for seventeenth-century astrological axioms and techniques. Michael Hunter and Annabel Gregory's editorship of the 'astrological diary'[9] of Samuel Jeake (1652-1699) also provided additional firsthand accounts of astrological practice which, in contrast to Josten's

---

9   M. Hunter and A. Gregory (eds.), *An astrological diary of the seventeenth century : Samuel Jeake of Rye*, 1652-1699 (Oxford, 1988).

Ashmole volumes, came from a practitioner whose religion, influenced by Puritan and nonconformist ideas, did not always seem to sit comfortably with his astrology. This offers particularly fascinating insight into contemporary opinions on the interrelations and delineations of astrology, magic and religion. Patrick Curry's *Power and Prophecy* (Cambridge, 1989) readdressed the political functions of English astrology in this period. Curry's book categorised astrology into 'elite' (Royalist) and 'democratic' (Parliamentarian) types, analysing politicisation of astrological conceptions of the proper nature and operation of the universe – as both sides of the civil war attempted to justify their politics by appeal to astrological understanding of nature, to insist either that "inferiors obey superiors" or that "the stars incline but do not compel". The political nature of astrology (and the astrological politics of nature itself) was explored through emphasising the magical universe's interrelations of microcosm and macrocosm.

Another important work to consider the interrelation of politics and nature was Ottavia Niccoli's *Prophecy and People in Renaissance Italy* (Princeton, 1990) which considered the political and cultural impact of early modern prophecy as a combination of various magical as well as religious comprehensions of natural processes. While this book's focus is sixteenth-century Italy, Niccoli's observations about the intersection of politics, humans and nature in prophecy are also useful insights for considering seventeenth-century English astrology. Further, far more detailed assessment of astrology's contemporary political utility came from Ann Geneva's *Astrology and the Seventeenth Century Mind* (Manchester, 1995), which examined in great detail the 'language of the stars' as used by England's most famous astrologer of the time, William Lilly (1602-1681). Geneva utilised her deep reading of Lilly's work to emphasise the cryptographic importance of astrological symbolism in covert political assessment and criticism, deeply expanding upon the explicit propaganda value identified by Rusche. Geneva emphasised a rational function of astrology as an interpretive, analytical and critical tool or 'multi-layered symbolic language system'[10] of seventeenth-century English political activity, thereby also stressing the necessity of astrological interpreters and code-breakers, and developing consideration of the transformative effects of astrological knowledge.

The medical dimensions of early modern astrology have been considerably advanced by two more recent works. Lauren Kassell's *Medicine and Magic in Elizabethan London: Simon Forman – Astrologer, Alchemist, and Physician* (Oxford, 2005) presented a deep reading of Forman's case histories, notebooks and many unfinished works which offered fresh perspectives on early modern attitudes and practices concerning physician-patient relations (specifically regarding gender and gynaecology), as well as exploring how astrology related to the myriad magical practices of Simon Forman (1552-1611). David Lederer's *Madness, Religion and the State in Early Modern Europe: A Bavarian Beacon* (Cambridge, 2006) presented and analysed a variety of early modern ideas concerning the interrelations of body, mind and soul. Lederer's book significantly develops MacDonald's early work on diagnosis and treatment of impaired mental faculties during this period, including greater assessment of spiritual afflictions and the Christian moral casuistry that often accompanied them. Like Niccoli's *Prophecy and People*, Lederer's work offers us valuable comparisons and commonalities to be drawn from a wider European perspective on astrology's role in restoring and maintaining physical, mental and spiritual well-being.

---

10   Ann Geneva, *Astrology and the Seventeenth Century Mind* (Manchester, 1995), p. 176.

Two works by Owen Davies have also recently developed important strands within the history of astrology. *Popular Magic: Cunning-folk in English History* (New York, 2007) has located a firm astrological basis in the magical activities of village wizards and wise-women – reminding us that astrology did not merely inform high ceremonial court magic or the summoning of angels, but was also the most ubiquitous element throughout the magical activities of "common" practitioners. *Popular Magic* also provided snapshots of the clients and patients of astrological practitioners, and glimpses of their concerns, problems and expectations for magical services on offer. Davies' *Grimoires: A History of Magic Books* (Oxford, 2009) likewise presented study of astrology as an important element of magic, exploring links between the history of magic and of print. Contributing to the work begun in Capp's *Astrology and the Popular Press*, it focuses on Europe as a whole over an incredibly broad period of time (from the ancient world to the 1960s), offering an expansive context within which to discuss links between astrology, magic and written text.

This historiography highlights three key factors in our conceptions of astrology: firstly, the relation between magic and astrology; secondly, notions about astrology functioning as a practice as well as knowledge; and finally, how astrology has been examined as contributing to understanding environmental, political and social contexts of early modern England. It is the intention of this book to draw upon extant scholarship to develop and explore our understanding of these ideas – to not only consider how people of the seventeenth century comprehended and used astrology, but also to consider how historians have presented and analysed it.

AREAS OF STUDY

There are a number of topics related to, but not specifically addressing, astrology that this book does not cover. It does not discuss astrology's functions relating to the emerging scientific experimental methodology, and does not investigate astronomy or meteorology. Nor does this book examine debates about determinism and free will, or contemporary discussion over astrology's legitimacy.

Although it seeks to examine astrology's interrelations with occult philosophy and magical practice, it does not look at any of the massively diverse and important cultural impacts of witchcraft and witch trials. Finally, this book does not assess factors behind the decline of astrology in the final years of the early modern period.

The focus of this book is upon the expectations, services and practical applications of astrology in seventeenth-century England. It analyses *how* astrology was used, and what it was used *for*. It examines both analysis and management of celestial influence, and explores links between divination and enchantment activities within astrology. This study of the functions of astrology should be distinguished from study of the functions of *belief in* astrology. The purpose of this book is to offer an understanding of early modern astrological thought and action as it was used, rather than explaining or excusing it from the vantage of hindsight. For these reasons, I have considered astrology on its own terms at the height of its popularity to explore what people did with astrology – to understand the functions astrology fulfilled.

In order to assess astrology's broad and far-reaching functions in seventeenth-century England, I have divided this book into three main chapters, prefaced by a brief introduction to the premises, mechanisms and techniques of astrology. Chapter 2 considers astrology's broadest functions in assessing human existence in relation to the environment. It analyses how astrology constructed human meaning for time, history and nature. It stresses the unifying capacity of astrology to explore and manage fundamental occult interrelations posited to underlie existence. Chapter 3 narrows assessment of astrological functions by focusing on political contexts for astrological theory and practice. It analyses astrology's functions in relation to prophecy, political analysis and propaganda. It also deals with astrology's considerations of political organisation as but one level of complexity in a unifying ontological and epistemological system. Chapter 4 further narrows this book's analysis of astrological utility, considering astrological understanding of human societies and individuals, as well as the links between the two. It deals with the variety of services astrological practitioners offered in their personal consultations, and considers the wide range of magical activities that astrology supported and cross-pollinated.

PREMISES

It may seem bizarre to modern sensibilities that astrology should have such an impact and significance. The study of astrology therefore makes an important contribution to the history of early modern England by seeking to not simply "explain away" but to understand astrological worldviews. Such study delivers early modern astrological practitioners, their clients and their wider audience from a condescending appraisal of astrology as fundamentally irrational or nonsensical. As has been pointed out, 'logic of whatever kind... contains no guarantees as to the correctness of premises'[11], and to call astrological practice irrational or

---

11   Patrick Curry, *Power and Prophecy* (Cambridge, 1989), p. 14.

illogical is to do it a great disservice. In order to understand astrology on its own terms, we must look at its underlying mechanics. Astrology was the theory and practice of analysing and managing influences of celestial forces on human affairs. It rested upon a number of premises shared with magical thinking. According to infamous occult philosopher Heinrich Cornelius Agrippa von Nettesheim (1486-1535), magic is, *inter alia*, 'the differing, and agreement of things with themselves.'[12] The following principles are astrological theories on how phenomena interact with one another.

The central notion of astrology contends that as celestial bodies move in the heavens, so too do earthly events unfold in corresponding ways. This idea is described by the Emerald Tablet of Hermes Trismegistus, which states: 'That wch is below is like that wch is above [;] that wch is above is like yt wch is below'.[13] This is the notion of an interlinking macrocosm and microcosm – of an interconnected universe where the smallest parts and processes are accurate portrayals of the largest and vice versa. This principle or theory, that the massive machinations of the cosmos might illustrate and correspond to the relatively tiny actions and events upon Earth, is the main foundation of astrology. Astrology was considered 'a rational attempt to map the state of the heavens and to interpret that map in the context of that "cosmic sympathy" which makes man an integral part of the universe.'[14]

---

12 Heinrich Cornelius Agrippa, *Three Books of Occult Philosophy*, ed. by D. Tyson (St. Paul, 2004), p. 5.

13 B.J.T. Dobbs, 'Newton's Commentary on the Emerald Tablet of Hermes Trismegistus' in Ingrid Merkel & Allen G. Debus (eds.), *Hermeticism and the Renaissance* (Washington, 1988), p. 182-91.

14 S.J. Tester, *A History of Western Astrology* (Bury St. Edmunds, 1987), p. 18.

From this notion of a basic interconnection of all things, several further principles can be outlined. The first is *'similitude'* – that 'everything moves, and turns itself to its like, and inclines that to itself with all its might.'[15] In similitude, things are connected because they share fundamental essences. The occult properties of things are imbued at their creation 'through the rays of the stars'.[16] Indeed, astrology works precisely because all things are thought to be imbued with astral properties or "virtues". The principle of *contagion* or *exposure* assumed that this occult virtue could be transferred between things. This transfer of 'vertue' or occult properties through exposure plays a vital role in understanding why accurate astronomical data was necessary for the setting of an astrological figure – as the stars moved through the heavens, their influence waxed and waned.

Heavily connected with similitude is the principle of *sympathy*.[17] This states that even things that are not alike, but which might nevertheless "agree", also share a link. Magnetism was considered in terms of sympathy – 'that attractive inclination, which loadstone hath upon iron'.[18] Conversely, there is a notion that certain things also share effects upon each other by their "disagreement" or *antipathy* – that unlike can *compel* unlike. Agrippa refers the popularisation of these ideas to Heraclitus, who 'professed that all things were made by enmity and friendship.'[19] This way of looking at the world is characteristic of a holistic view

---

15   Agrippa, *Three Books*, p. 46.

16   Ibid.

17   'such kind of attractions by the mutual correspondency of things amongst themselves' Ibid, p. 110, p. 111 n.2.

18   Ibid, p. 40 n. 1.

19   Ibid, p. 52.

of an interconnected universe – phenomena are defined or considered by their opposites as well as their likenesses. The idea of antipathy was further complicated by conceptions of common enemies in the natural world. Therefore, the turtledove and the parrot were considered to be magically "friendly" to each other, despite their only connection being a shared antipathy to foxes.[20] These contrasting and opposite forces of sympathy and antipathy play an important astrological role in characterising the relations between planets and the zodiac.

These are some of the key astrological principles positing *why* astrology worked. To understand *how* astrology was thought to work, we must examine specific astrological structures – the conceptions of the elements and humours, planets, signs and houses of the heavens. These are the specific structures that astrological activity utilises, as opposed to the mechanics of magical axioms by which such work is done.

The planets were the seven classical observable celestial bodies, which included the Sun and Moon, while the zodiac was a band of twelve astrological signs which made an annual orbit through the sky. The planets and signs were collectively referred to as "the stars". The 'Houses of the Heavens' were specific fixed areas of the sky, used to give a position to the stars. The planets represented a particular force or experience (i.e. Venus representing love), the zodiac signs represented how that force manifested (i.e. Aries represented courage and 'impetuosity'[21]), and the houses each signified a particular area of life (such as "Possessions",

---

20   Ibid, p. 55 n. 11.

21   K.M. Briggs, *The Last of the Astrologers* (London, 1974), p. xiv.

"Children" or "Career"[22]) that this force would affect.[23] Each planet had sympathetic and antipathetic relations with the signs – when a planet shared a position with a sign it "ruled", the planet's influence was amplified. Conversely, detrimental signs impeded planetary influence. The planets were also linked through sympathies and antipathies with each other.[24] Astrologers could find further meaning by assessing particular configurations or relation of planets to one another – called *aspects*. Some aspects, such as the *trine*, were considered favourable, whilst the *square* or *quartile* was considered ill-fated. Crucially, the *conjunction* configuration could be understood as beneficient or malevolent depending on interpretation.

The signs were also afforded an elemental identity – three signs to each of the four classical elements of Fire, Water, Air and Earth. So the signs Aries, Leo and Sagittarius were considered to exert a hot and dry Fiery influence. This is significant to our studies because early modern humoural theories of 'the body are also based on elemental analysis – the four humours (choler, phlegm, blood and bile[25]) correspond to the four elements. Humoural theory posited

---

22 'Lucrum', 'Genitor' and 'Regnum' respectively, as translated from volume III of Robert Fludd's *Utriusque Cosmi majoris scilicet et minoris metaphysica atque technica historia in duo volumina secundum cosmi differentiam divisa* (Oppenheim and Frankfurt, 1617-1626), p. 76.

23 Stephen Skinner, *Terrestrial Astrology: Divination by Geomancy* (London, 1980), p. 210.

24 William Lilly, *Christian Astrology* (London, 1647), p. 68-83.

25 Bile, or black bile, was also called 'melancholy' – a term that, confusingly, was also used to denote the kind of natural humoural composition of an individual (or 'temperament') which had a stable predomination of black bile, *and also* to refer to the pathological imbalance of the humours with an excess of black bile. See Angus Gowland, 'The Problem of Early Modern Melancholy', *Past & Present*, 191, (May 2006), p. 77-120.

that 'man's body was made up of the four elements and the four qualities held, in good health, in a proper balance, or harmony.'[26] The four immutable qualities mentioned above are the properties of the mutable elements: hot, cold, dry, and moist. The distinction between elements and qualities explained how universal phenomena were capable of both change and stability. So a beaker of water (made up of the Watery element which possessed cold and moist qualities) when put on a flame to boil would exchange the cold for heat, producing steam or air (the hot and moist element); yet the fundamental qualities themselves, although swapping to produce different elemental functions, would not alter. Humoural medicine, treatments to bring the humours from a *dyscrasia* (literally "bad mixture") into healthy balance, underlies most physic practiced during the early modern period, both by licensed, educated doctors and the multitude of "irregular" medical practitioners; apothecaries, cunning-folk, astrologer-physicians, *et al*. As we shall see, astrology played an important role in attempts to aid patients by balancing their humours.

Finally, we should be aware of the techniques commonly used in seventeenth-century English astrology. Perhaps most iconic are *nativities*, charts mapping the stars' positions at the point of a person's birth. The "native" was considered intimately linked to these configurations – a nativity could be used to assess an individual's personality and destiny. Another common astrological technique was the *horary* figure – a snapshot of the heavens which would offer divinatory answers by interpreting the stars' positions at the time the question was asked. Astrological practitioners also drew up *elections*, which assessed the best time to begin a journey, project or enterprise so as to best

---

26   Tester, p. 61.

utilise astrological influences for one's benefit. These are far from the only techniques that astrological practitioners utilised, but specific procedures and practices will be dealt with in the following three chapters, addressing the environmental, political and social functions of seventeenth-century English astrology.

CHAPTER 2
THE ENVIRONMENTAL

WHEN ASSESSING TYPES OF ASTROLOGY, WE ARE generally presented with a division into two approaches. It has been considered that astrology has 'experienced a conflict between more magical and more rationalistic strands throughout [its] history... between a more divinatory and more rationalistic tradition.'[27] This rationalistic tradition has been called "natural astrology", and is most often characterised as the strand of astrology concerned with renovating astrological practice through empirical experimentation. It is the *astrologia sana* of Francis Bacon (1561-1626), supported by contemporaries such as Samuel Jeake and astrologer John Gadbury (1627-1704), which 'saw astrology as comparable to other forms of natural causation'.[28] Empirical evidence was to be used to reason conclusions about the operation of the universe. This supposedly more "rationalistic" approach to astrology streamlined the detailed considerations of astral influences which characterised other more Neo-platonic approaches, and instead emphasised simpler analysis of birth charts.[29] This further emphasised the consideration of astrology as a natural causation of phenomena – a central consideration in the natural philosophy of astrology. Much has already been made of this area of astrological theory and

---

27   M. Hunter and A. Gregory (eds.), p. 13.

28   Ibid, p. 14.

29   Ibid.

practice in histories of science and proto-science – Patrick
Curry considers the 'natural law-like determinism' of this
approach to be a foundation for interest in astrology from
such historians as Lynn Thorndike and Otto Neugebauer.[30]
This "natural astrology" is considered to have de-emphasised
more occult or magical practices such as horary astrology.
However, natural astrology also refers to certain astrological
practices and applications concerning the natural world
itself, such as forecast of weather, harvest and epidemics.
We should therefore begin by distinguishing the approach
or discourse which can be called the natural philosophy of
astrology, from the actual practices of natural or "nature
astrology" itself. This book will not concern itself with the
natural philosophy of astrology – the pursuit of astrology
that sought 'to refine the techniques and test the principles
of astrology by careful empiricism'[31] – but it will look at
the actual applications and practices of natural astrology
because, as we shall see, they share much common ground
with other predictive astrological techniques typically
depicted as "magical".

This book puts forward a broad working definition for
natural astrology, as the practice of deciphering information
from the stars regarding "the natural world" – agriculture,
weather, disease and so on. However astrology also considered
events of the human microcosmic world a part of the natural
macrocosmic world. Therefore astrology concerned itself
with mass movements in human society, assessing them as
expressions of natural processes. Francis Bacon defined his

---

30   Curry, p. 8: citing Thorndike, 'The True Place of Astrology in the
      History of Science', *Isis*, 46 (1955), p. 273-78, and 'Neugebauer (1953)',
      which may refer to Neugebauer, 'On the 'Hippopede' of Eudoxus.'
      Scripta Mathematica, 19 (1953), p. 225-29, although this is not listed in
      his bibliography. See Curry, p. 171 n. 23, 223.

31   Hunter and Gregory, p. 15.

naturalistic 'sane astrology', for example, to be concerned with 'all commotions or great innovations of things natural *and* civil.'[32] Natural astrological practice was therefore in most cases a generalised form of speculative and predictive activity, and not so far removed from the expressly political character of judicial divinatory astrology.[33]

TIME

The widest environmental context within which to consider human agency is existence and action in time as well as space. As Proclus observed, 'time is the number of the motion of the celestial bodies'.[34] While astronomical observation of the movements of celestial bodies was a widely used means of *measuring* the passage of time even into the seventeenth century,[35] astrology played a significant role in early modern *understanding* of time. Astrology offers symbolic meaning for observable phenomena to not only mark but provide meaning for the passage of time. To say, for example, that the Sun "enters" Aries[36] (as it does at the start of spring to begin the new astrological year) is to say that the fiery nature of Aries acts as an energetic reawakening of nature from its winter slumber into a new spring beginning.

---

32   *The works of Francis Bacon*, (ed. Basil Montagu), III, p. 132; cited in Tester, p. 222 [emphasis added]. Bacon specified the new astrology would study 'comets, ...meteors, inundations, droughts, heats, frosts, earth-quakes, fiery eruptions, winds, great rains, the seasons of the year, plagues, epidemic diseases, plenty, famine, wars, seditions, sects, transmigrations of people...'

33   For more on this judicial divinatory astrology, see Chapter 3.

34   Agrippa, *Three Books*, p. 238 n 2; citing Proclus, *On Motion*, 2.

35   For more on early modern time measurement, see Thomas, p. 395.

36   i.e. as the band of the zodiac moves across the sky, Aries comes to occupy the position in the sky from where the sun rises.

A particular period of time and the events occurring within that period were not considered merely arbitrary or coincidental but closely interlinked. The changing seasonal cycles affected flora (observed in their specific flowering and harvest times), fauna (in animal mating seasons) and, most obviously, the seasonal climates. To consider this in a slightly different manner, the effect of winter upon nature (i.e. upon the world *and* humanity) occurred because such influence was instilled by virtue of winter's particular astrological identity. As the wild natural world was clearly regulated by specific timing, so too human events and experience were thought to be linked to time. Astrology offered a cyclical conception of the processes of time upon nature – a nature that united the activities of people and their environment.

Astrology's scope with regards to time was universal – it mapped the entirety of human and cosmic existence. Astrology linked small divisions of time important for everyday human life (such as days and hours) with the vast spans of millennia into one continuous and universal astrological scope. It did so through cyclical conceptions inspired by observable planetary revolution – small cycles of celestial orbits constructing ever grander cycles towards a single period measuring the entire span of the universe. It provided meaning for the duration of all existence, and to the processes unfolding to the very end of time and the cosmos itself.

This astrological period of an entire cosmos-length is illustrated by the concept of the Great Year – a Platonic idea that the universe literally repeated its events and various unfolding history every 36,000 years.[37] It has been suggested that 'underneath... later theories of cyclical history lies a shadow astrological tradition... whose continuity remains

---

37   Bernard Capp, Astrology and the Popular Press: English Almanacs
      1500-1800 (London, 1979), p. 223.

unbroken from 8th century Islamic theorists to William Lilly in the seventeenth century.'[38] Such an astrologically derived idea of eternal recurrence was not agreeable with later Christian doctrine; partly because it obscured the act of Creation at the beginning, and partly because it denied the permanency of any divine Judgement or Redemption at the end.[39] Therefore this universal cycle-length, originally representing the endlessness of the cosmos, came to be understood by the 'one-cycle cosmological system[s]' of Judaism and Christianity as representing the life-span of the whole of creation.[40] So astrology ultimately helped encode, eschatologically speaking, the point at which time itself would stop. In many ways, astrological speculation on the end-times was a logical extension of the idea of general divination by the movement of the stars. However rather than predict likelihoods of particular events, or even outline broad trends of fortune, the eschatology of speculative astrology attempted to discern the nature of the final conclusion of *all* affairs of the cosmos. It attempted to comprehend the mechanisms underlying the unfolding and completion of destiny. It is from this position that astrology presents a unique contribution to eschatology, periodisation, and the philosophy of history.

By the seventeenth century, overt Christian symbolism had come to take prominence in eschatological speculation.[41] Yet astrology was still an important component in considering the end-times. In the opening of *The Bloody Almanack* for 1643,

38   Geneva, p. 122.

39   Ibid, p. 120-22.

40   Ibid.

41   For more on early modern millenarianism and conceptions of apocalypse, see Bernard Capp, *The Fifth Monarchy Men: a study in seventeenth-century English millenarianism* (London, 1972).

astrologer John Booker (1602-1667) advanced a periodisation
of the history of Christianity, beginning with the later life of
Christ. This is based on interpretation of symbols from the
book of Revelation, namely, that the seven seals mentioned
therein mark seven-year periods by which 'you shall find the
effect of every seale to be performed within the seven years
of that seale; and so the harmony to be perfect betwixt those
seales and the just history.'[42] Booker notes that in the initial
'sixt[h] seven yeers [which would begin 71 AD], as the Text
saith, there was a great quake, and the Sun was black as sack-
cloth of haire, and the Moon was like to blood, and even so
after the yeare of *Christ* 64 a great change and defection came
on all estates of the Roman Empire'.[43] Booker's almanac
utilised scriptural quotation to form a historical theory and
cited celestial phenomena for its proof. There are many other
Biblical examples of Christian recuperation and utility of older
astrological ideas about celestial phenomena presaging both
the end-times and serious times of crisis.[44] An apt articulation
of the combination of astrology and Christian eschatology
comes from minister and astrologer Christopher Ness (1621-
1705), who reasoned that 'if so many prodigys attended
Christs' passion, surely many more may attend his Return in
Glory and the end of the World, many strange conjunctions
in Heaven, Earth and Sea.'[45] Throughout the seventeenth
century astrological, biblical and historical concepts were
fused into a single "astro-historical-eschatological" analysis.

---

42   John Booker, *The Bloody Almanack* (London, 1642), p. 1.

43   Ibid, p. 1-2, quoting from Revelation 6:12.

44   See Isaiah 13:10, Matthew 24:29, Luke 21:25, Joel 2:10, Joel 2:31, Acts
      2:20; and Joshua 10:13, 1 Corinthians 15:41, Ezekiel 32:7 and Luke
      23:44-5.

45   Christopher Ness, *An Astrological and Theological Discourse upon the
      present Great Conjunction* (London, 1682), p. 41.

PERIODISATION

The example above demonstrates two interlinked preoccupations of seventeenth-century English almanacs: complete histories of the world and periodisation. Almanacs frequently contained a brief timeline of the world's history.[46] As in Booker's account, the meaning of earthly events could be explained through astrological analysis of celestial phenomena. Yet use of astrology was not limited to providing proofs of crises throughout history. Astrology could also offer a comprehensive assessment of the underlying character of events, and link together these events through time as part of a continuous process. We should bear in mind that 'in a framework which strove to understand human affairs through the influence of recurring planetary conjunctions, "revolution" [as a cycle or period of time] could suggest the end of time (and the beginning of a new time), which is not much different from saying that it suggested notions such as destiny and change.'[47] The predictable conjunctions of planets were often used to measure the passage of time and analyse the unfolding of history.[48] However, astrology's contribution to history was not merely to mark out periods of time conveniently. Astrology provided functions for modelling and understanding historical events and processes. It provided language, taxonomies, analogies, and underlying structural assumptions with which to analyse history, both human and universal. Capp advances this relation of history and astrology further still:

---

46   Such chronologies were 'one of the most common features of the Stuart almanac'. Capp, *Astrology and the Popular Press*, p. 215.

47   Ilan Rachum, 'The term 'Revolution' in Seventeenth-Century English Astrology', *History of European Ideas*, 18, No. 6 (1994), p. 870.

48   For more on the history of theories of conjunction prior to the seventeenth century, see Geneva, p. 118-140.

'Such speculations reflect, once again, the confidence that astrology, properly studied, could provide the key to universal understanding. History itself might become a branch of astrological science.'[49]

Almanac makers and astrologers utilised the revolutions of planets not only to periodise time but to structure these formalised periods into interlinking and meaningful durations. This astrological analysis provided information that could be pieced together to comprehend the fundamental mechanics of history. Indeed, it has already been noted that 'astrological doctrines about the recurrence of planetary conjunctions and their influence upon the course of affairs had helped to form the concept of a historical period.'[50]

Astrology connected scales of meaning for time and history using longer cycles carefully observed from shorter ones. When outlining the relatively frequent conjunctions of Saturn and Jupiter[51] in his *Astrological Discourse*, Christopher Heydon (1561-1623) noted that over the twenty years between conjunctions, 'those Planets are moved from the place of their former Conjunctions 8 signs [and therefore still occurring in signs of the same elemental identity], and almost 3 degrees, which excess of 3 degrees is the cause why after 10 Conjunctions they pass from one *Triplicity* [a set of three signs of the same elemental identity] to another'. Because each sign occupies 30° of the total 360° of the Zodiac, every tenth time around the conjunction would have moved a total of 30° and thus occur in a sign of a different elemental identity. From these ten conjunctions

49   Capp, *Astrology*, p. 224.

50   Thomas, p. 386.

51   Every '19 *Aegyptian* years, 318 days, and 13 hours'. Christopher Heydon, *An Astrological Discourse* (London, 1650), p. 69.

we get 'one *Triplicity* [cycle, which] continueth 198 equal years, 265 days (the intercalary day of every fourth year [i.e. leap year] omitted) and 10 hours.' Finally therefore the grand 'Revolution of *all* the [four elemental] *Triplicities* is finished but only once in 794 equal years, 331 days and 16 hours.'[52] While these irregular astrological periods of time might at first appearance seem to demonstrate somewhat imperfectly balanced celestial mechanics, these very irregularities in fact allowed the construction of intricate cycles-within-cycles, such as the schema above. This lent a sense of fundamental connection between long-term movements of the universe and the shorter-term motions. It tied together the events observable within a human lifetime (such as the Saturn-Jupiter conjunction every twenty years) with those of a far more universal scale, such as the return of the conjunction to exactly the same point at which it had occurred nearly 795 years ago.

Astrological periodisation offers an understanding of early modern conceptions of an 'overall framework of history'.[53] Royalist astrologer George Wharton (1617-1681) considered five hundred to seven hundred year periods as important historical epochs. He explains that history is made of 'sundry changes and Translations of Kingdomes, whilst these or these Planets Raigne, and beare Rule with others'.[54] Specifically, he appealed to astrological effect on the human biology of successive generations. Wharton claimed that empires generally existed for this five- to seven-century period

---

52   Ibid.

53   Capp, *Astrology*, p. 223.

54   George Wharton, Hemeroscopeion Anni aerae, 1653. *Presenting the English and Roman Kalendar, Planetary Motions, Passions and Positions, Meteorologicall Observations, Chronologicall Collections, and Judgements Astrologicall, &c.* (London, 1653), p. 35.

because successive generations of humans become weaker than their forefathers, culminating in the sixth generation.[55] As the planets cycled around and humans became weaker until their next astral infusion of vitality, so too our empires waned and collapsed, or else were overthrown by a newly-invigorated generation. History, for Wharton, is made by people, but people shaped by the heavens.

William Lilly, arguably seventeenth-century England's most famous astrologer, made extensive use of 'Tritemius'[56] in describing an astrological periodisation of the history of humanity based upon cycling governorships of planetary angels. These angels were considered the *Secundarian Intelligences* instituted by God and 'appointed as Presidents of the 7 Planets'.[57] Such angels were an important link between astrology and Christianity, providing an integrated system of early modern analysis that utilised both astrological and Christian symbolism. This periodisation endowed its epochs with planetary characteristics. The first era, beginning in 'the first year of the World', was governed by the angel of Saturn and, as such, 'under his dominion men were rude, and did cohabite together in desert and uncouth places'.[58] This idea anthropomorphised eras by creating an angelic figurehead or, in the Platonic sense, an ideal character of that age. History, both scriptural and actual, is fitted to astrological symbolism, creating further explanation and

---

55   Ibid, p. 34.

56   Johannes Trithemius (1462-1516), German abbot and occultist. Lilly does not specify the work of Trithemius from which he draws this analysis.

57   God being, of course, 'the first *Intellect*'. William Lilly, *The World's Catastrophe* (London, 1647), p. 42.

58   Lilly cites the proof of this 'manifest out of the Text in Genesis.' Ibid.

meaning for remarkable events. This notion also offers an underlying common character or motivating force to the people and events of an era. The Great Flood is explained as divine refutation of a 'wantonness of life in men' that occurred during the rule of the angel of Venus, Anael. Blame is not laid upon Anael as an absolutely corrupting influence though – it is noted that 'Under the Regiment of this Angell, men began to be more Civilized'.[59] Astrology once more outlined the inclinations, persuasions and predispositions that encourage the particular behaviour and mentality of people within a given period of time.

HUMAN TIME

Astrology was not limited to providing meaning and understanding to time on universal or historical scales. The zodiac signs divided the year into twelfths, each with a particular character derived from their element and qualities – perhaps astrology's most resilient idea, surviving down to modern times. A collection of three signs made up every season, expressing a unique seasonal astrological identity.[60] Astrological handbooks and treatises provided incredibly detailed descriptions of the correspondences of the signs – what plants, animals, places and types of people were associated with each of the zodiacal taxons and divisions of the year – and almanacs were full of advice detailing which months were most favourable for particular activities.[61] This kind of interpretation of month-long periods was the recognisable staple of the astrologer's craft.

---

59   Ibid.

60   i.e. spring (consisting of Aries, Taurus and Gemini) therefore consists of a Fiery beginning, an Airy middle and an Earthy ending.

61   See also the section on election, Chapter 2.

It helped encode a person's experiences of themselves and other people using a twelve-part taxonomy of personality traits, as well as providing a complex means to understand how (via roving planetary position against the zodiac) dynamic human individuals were constantly changing. It encouraged a meaningful link between an individual and the natural world. Astrology emphasised the importance of one's precise time of birth as both a unique point in time, mapping exact positions of celestial bodies, and as a part of a continuous and universal spectrum – a grand cosmic process of expression that was happening *with* rather than *to* us.

Astrology also provided a wider significance to quotidian human times such as days and hours. The seven days of the week were given planetary signatures corresponding to their names.[62] Early modern magic-users even referred to weekdays in their writing by using planetary glyphs.[63] The planetary character of the days regulated both ordinary and magical activities. The magical system of the *Heptameron* broke magical operations into seven categories, each based on the nature of a planet, which were only to be performed on the relevant day.[64] As well as investing each day with a particular planetary character or energy, each day was given over to the guardianship of a planetary archangel. The *Theomagia* of occultist John Heydon (b. 1629, d. in or around 1670) details seven planetary "Spirits" or '*Ideas*' which similarly rule the

---

62   i.e. Saturday as "Saturn's day".

63   See diaries of Ashmole and Jeake: C.H. Josten, Elias Ashmole and Hunter & Gregory (eds.), *An Astrological Diary*.

64   Agrippa, *Fourth Book of Occult Philosophy*, trans. R. Turner (London, 1655), p. 94. For example, operations of Mars were carried out with the intention of creating martial or violent effect, and were performed on a Tuesday. For more on the Heptameron, see below.

days.[65] So as the weekdays cycled, they reflected and were reflected by a larger celestial ordering – the movements of the planets and shared governance of angelic forces.

Even divisions of an individual day were afforded astrological importance, each day being divided into periods attributed to a planetary ruler. The astrological identity of these 'artificial hours'[66] is explained by John Heydon ("quoting" Agrippa):

'about the times of choosing the planetary hours; for almost all Astrologers divide all that space of time from the Sun-rising to setting into twelve equal parts, and call them the twelve hours of the day... and then distribute each of those hours to every one to the Planets according to the order of successions'.[67]

Astrology characterised each hour[68] as carrying an inherent significance, providing an astrological undercurrent of meaning for each mundane utility of daily timing. The planetary hours were not based upon the position of the stars at that time of the day, but upon a symbolic astrological sequence. We may therefore note here a clear separation

---

65 The Spirit of Mercury Taphthartharath, for example, 'Governeth Wednesday'. John Heydon, *Theomagia* (London, 1664), p. 42.

66 Dividing the day into 'artificial hours' was a practice from at least the Elizabethan period that had 'still survived in popular usage' into the seventeenth century. Thomas, p. 394.

67 J. Heydon, *Theomagia*, p. 178; verbatim from Agrippa, chapter XXXIV (*Three Books*, p. 371). The planets were assigned 'giving always the first hour of the day to the Lord of that day, then to every one by order'. This 'order' of the ruling Lords is the so-called Chaldean order of ascending speeds of the planets, Saturn deemed slowest and the Moon fastest.

68 In fact, an exact twelfth of the day's sunlight.

between the symbolism of astrology and the observations of astronomy. The latter certainly aided knowledge of long durations of time through measurement, but the former provided means to interpret or understand time on a more quotidian level.

Knowledge of these hours facilitated magical action, most notably in the carefully timed construction of magical talismans that would "soak up" astral influence. So Agrippa describes 'the operations of Mars [:] they made an image in the hour of Mars, Mars ascending in... Aries'.[69] The timing combined the planetary hours with actual astronomical observation – in this case, when the planet Mars was in Aries in the heavens – and as such there was not only a day but an hour deemed most suitable for operations of this kind. The casting of metal seals attributed to particular zodiac signs had similar instructions – the seal of Taurus must be cast when 'the *Sun* being in *Taurus,* which every yeer happens about the eighth day of *April*.'[70] Ashmole used planetary hours to cast many sigils to contain astral influence for creating magical effects.[71] At precisely 11 a.m., 2.17, 3.15 and 4.30 p.m. on 18th July 1650 as '[Saturn] and [Mars] continued in the 8th house', Ashmole 'cast off in Lead' several sigils 'against Fleas, Flyes, Caterpillars, & Toades'.[72] In Ashmole's magical repellents we see that astrology could be used to not only locate the individual as a significant part of the cosmos, but also aid that individual in achieving effect upon the world – even if that effect was something as mundane as warding off

---

69 Aries being ruled by Mars. Agrippa, *Three Books*, p. 385.

70 *Paracelsus Of Supreme Mysteries of Nature*, trans. R Turner (London, 1655), p. 139.

71 Josten, p. 1694; citing MS. Ashm. 421, f. 139.

72 MS Ashm. 431, ff. 121-2, cited in Josten, p. 537.

unwanted domestic pests. One could be provided this aid by mapping the astrological forces that underlay phenomenal existence and, combined with magical principles and structures of meaning, one was thus offered the ability to affect as well as analyse events. Furthermore, astrology's epic scope stretched from the end of the universe to dealing with some of the most material of domestic nuisances.[73] This ability to affect events, made possible by magical premises such as sympathy and contagion, nevertheless hinged upon understanding fundamental astrological correspondences that linked phenomena – for example, Saturn and Mars affecting infestations of vermin – and acting at an exact point in time so as to best harness the forces of astral influence permeating existence.

Sigils and other charms 'thought to preserve the favourable planetary influences and to place them permanently at the disposal of the wearer' are especially important to a central argument of this book: that, as Capp puts it, 'magic here clearly fused with astrology'.[74] I would like to affirm this statement, but to take from it a slightly different interpretation. I would argue that instead of seeing sigils as merely one form of astrological activity that fused with magic, as opposed to other "scientific" forms of astrology, sigils mark a point on an interdisciplinary astrological-magical spectrum at which it becomes most clear to modern thinkers that astrology itself was fused with magic.

73   See also Chapter 4.

74   Capp, *Astrology*, p. 21.

THE HEPTAMERON

The *Heptameron*[75] provides a particularly useful case study of astrological time-specific magic. The *Heptameron* employs a magical circle inscribed with planetary angel names, as well as incantations that call upon specific planetary angels of the days.[76] The type of effect one hoped to create by conjuring and commanding angels was dependent upon planetary rulerships of the days. Operations of Venus (which were performed to 'excite men, and incline them to luxury; to reconcile enemies through luxury; and to make marriages; to allure men to love women; to cause, or take away infirmities; and to do all things which have motion') must be made on a Friday.[77] The actual inscriptions of the circle vary according to the time of year, the day and the hour of the magical operation itself. One must write, *inter alia*, the magical name of the hour in which the ritual is performed, the name of the Angel of that hour, 'the name of the Angel that ruleth that day wherein you do the work, and the names of his ministers', the occult name of the season, as well as those for the Sun, Moon and Earth in that season.[78] These names were not merely written to draw astral influence; they were intoned as part of a conjuration of spiritual intelligences. Spoken as well as written expression formed an essential part of effect-creating knowledge. The circle forms a crib-sheet

---

75   Also called 'The Magical Elements of Peter de Abano' in Agrippa's *Fourth Book of Occult Philosophy*. It seems reasonably accepted that this work is not that of Peter de Abano; nor indeed is it wholly agreed upon that the *Fourth Book* is even by Agrippa.

76   'imploring... all the Names and Spirits written in the Circle...'. Agrippa, *Fourth Book*, p. 82.

77   Ibid, p. 101

78   Ibid, p. 74-5.

detailing the correct order and passwords for the granting of requests or demands made of spirits able to assist the operator at the specific time of operation. The magic circle of the *Heptameron* is therefore intricately tied to timing, to the extent that it sacralises the very encoding of the time of operation into an address to active angelic agents. In addition, ritual tools like a pentacle were made observing astrological conditions[79], and the ceremony itself was always to be performed with the Moon at a particular position.[80] Astrology allowed the very timing of an act to consecrate that act and its effects.

CLIMATE

Astrology was considered crucial for analysing climate. Weather forecasts had an important place in seventeenth-century almanacs – an almanac without weather predictions was considered to be 'like a Pudding without Sewet, or a Christmas-pye without Plums.'[81] It was clearly a staple part of what readers wanted or expected, and meteorology was a common interest for astrologers.[82] Samuel Jeake certainly

79   It must be 'made in the day and hour of Mercury, the Moon increasing [i.e. waxing].' It should be noted that this pentacle was not a disk or stone, as the term is used by some modern magical practitioners (especially in traditions derived from the practices of the nineteenth-century Hermetic Order of the Golden Dawn or twentieth-century Wicca), but rather a decorated six-pointed star symbol 'written in parchment made of a kids skin.' Ibid, p. 79.

80   Ibid, p. 81.

81   Adam Martindale, *Country Almanack For the Year 1676* (London, 1676), sig. B 2; cited in Capp, *Astrology*, p. 63.

82   Ashmole apparently owned a copy of 'Dr Formans observacon for Raine', and also made copies of parts of 'Observations concerning the Weather Excerpted out of DR Napiers diary'; not to mention Ashmole's own 'Observations of the Weather, made at my House at South-

drew astrological figures for the times of new and full moons in order to decipher weather predictions from them.[83]

The astrological rules for weather prediction consisted of specific astrological configurations being thought to create (or at the very least presage) particular weather conditions.[84] Many almanac writers may well have been dubious about the accuracy of weather prediction, but still included astrological rules for how to do it.[85] Nevertheless, the planets, which moved in predictable cycles, were believed to directly affect the qualities and properties of the air.[86] By extension, such cycles must have also affected the weather. Weather prediction further exemplifies how astrology united and analysed phenomena, through consideration of cyclical influences as expressions of a dynamic universal system.

By understanding climate, one could take advantage of this knowledge, most obviously in agriculture. Almanacs frequently offered advice on the astrologically propitious times to 'plough, sow, geld animals or fell timber.'[87] Such agricultural usage of astrology was a simpler version than formal figure-casting, involving less mathematics. Astrologer and mathematician Henry Coley (1633-1704) suggested that all agricultural astrology needed was the zodiac sign that the

---

Lambert'. Geneva notes 'John Dee also kept extensive weather records which he correlated with astronomical data.' Geneva, pp. 78, 80.

83   Hunter and Gregory, p. 15-16.

84   i.e. 'the [conjunction] [quartile] or [opposition] of Mars and Venus in Aries, Leo, [or] Sagittarius [:] In Winter it causeth dry weather and drought'. Seth Partridge, *Synopsis* (London, 1656), sig. B2.

85   For example, 'even Gilden, who thought weather prediction 'lost labour', still printed the rules of weather prediction.' Capp, Astrology, p. 62; cites Gilden, 1616, sig. B3 and Gilden, 1624, sig. B2.

86   Thomas, p. 396.

87   Capp, *Astrology*, p. 63.

sun occupied and the phases of the moon.[88] Moon-lore, as a particular subset of astrology, offered optimum times for when land should be manured[89] and when to geld lambs.[90] Capp has gathered several examples of the use of astrological principles in gardening, farming and planting: even diarist John Evelyn (1620-1706), sceptical of judicial astrology, observed the "correct" moment to plant trees.[91] This should not really surprise us, given that plants, responding to annual temperature and moisture fluctuations, do genuinely germinate better when particular planting times are observed. Astrology offered a certain further depth of analysis of such natural phenomena.[92]

While agricultural election relied more on general knowledge of favourable periods than exact figures, the principles are identical. In searching for the most appropriate point in time to begin an endeavour, in order to take full advantage of the various astrological influences, most agricultural astrology was a form of election.[93] Agricultural astrology further affirms the advantage of humanity acting *as part of* their natural environment, in harmony with the annual rhythms of nature. Such affirmation attempts not only to explain the forces influencing the links between people and their landscape, crops and animals, but explores the best methods and practices to take full advantage of such forces. The power of the Moon in astrological agriculture should also be considered in terms of the magical images of

88   Ibid, p. 64; citing Coley (1679), sig. C7v-8.

89   Ibid, p. 63.

90   Ibid, p. 290.

91   Ibid, p. 289-90.

92   See also the section on election, Chapter 2.

93   See section on election, Chapter 2.

its *mansions*, which were particular celestial positions similar to the houses of the heavens. The Moon could operate as a charge for magical talismans to aid farming as well as a clock by which to tell planting-times. Agrippa lists images of the twenty-fourth and twenty-fifth mansions as being used, respectively, 'for the multiplying of herds and cattle' and 'for the preservation of trees and harvests'.[94]

Astrology had a strong interest in both prediction and explanation of outbreaks of epidemic. In early modern England, it was 'plausible for astrologers to predict disease and mortality since it was generally accepted that people's health was affected by the state of the air and that the air was influenced by the heavens.'[95] The credibility of such prediction might also be linked to the general notion that the weather itself operated in cycles of roughly 35 years.[96] Disease and weather conditions were already considered to be intimately related.[97] Certain predictable appearances of planets or conjunctions were thought to exert influence on the balance of humours and therefore contribute to ill-health. Capp has stated 'several compilers noted a possible correlation between conjunctions of Saturn and Jupiter, every 20 years, and outbreaks of plague.'[98] Richard Edlyn (1631-1677) made what turned out to be a correct prediction of the Great Plague of 1665 when he wrote in the previous year, 'great Plagues have also succeeded those preceding Conjunctions of the years 1603 and 1623 & that there are also two conjunctions of Saturn and Mars in the same sign; me

---

94   Agrippa, *Three Books*, p. 393.

95   Thomas, p. 396.

96   Capp, *Astrology*, p. 224.

97   Ibid, p. 185.

98   Ibid, p. 224.

thinks we have too great cause to fear an approaching Plague, and that a very great one, ere the year 1665 be expired.'[99] Similarly, John Gadbury posited 'a general cyclical theory... [that] the return of Saturn might be the cause of periodic outbreaks of plague' although Gadbury himself admitted his uncertainty about the complete validity of such a theory.[100] The predictability of planetary revolution, and the cyclical nature of phenomena they affected, allowed analyses of epidemics to look forwards, to forecast, instead of being restricted to documenting death-tolls.

Astrological speculation on epidemics occupies certain shared ground with traditions that considered particular days lucky or unlucky. One prime example would be the *dog days* of high summer, regarded as an intrinsically unlucky annual period, 'so called because of the influence of those stars called the Dog [Sirius, the Dog-Star]... beginning about the 20th day of July, and ending the 17th of August.'[101] The best approach was moderation during this period 'which had been linked since antiquity with the prevalence of disease.'[102] It was thought a particularly bad idea to take medicine of any kind during this period, or, indeed, to engage in sexual activity.[103] This last concern seems especially interesting, in that it presents an approach to the fundamentals of human existence that links individual reproduction with the wider environment. Astrologers mapped the positions of celestial

---

99   Richard Edlyn, *Prae-nuncius sydereus* (London, 1664), p. 42.

100 Capp, *Astrology*, p. 224; citing Gadbury (1675), sig. Ev-3v; Gadbury (1680), sig. B2.

101 Dorothy Partridge, *The woman's almanack, for the year 1694* (London, 1694), p. 5.

102 Capp, *Astrology*, p. 118.

103 Ibid, p. 64-65, 120-21.

bodies at one's time of birth in order to comprehend the astral influences that shaped an individual. Conception – the very biological causation of one's existence – is a logical beginning in analysing relationships between identity and environment. A sexual act is therefore placed within an environmental context and a point in time's continuum, uniquely shaped by astrological forces. As even animals restricted their mating to particular times, so too should humans (who were merely another expression of the natural world) be wary of the temporal context in which they acted. In this regard, the dog days acted as a sort of anti-election, a period in which it was *un*wise to begin a project, such as an erotic relationship or an attempt to conceive. Elections provide a further rationale to support ideas about lucky and unlucky days, as well as a framework for their analysis. Just as sexual activity was discouraged during the dog days, almanacs also offered, along with council on timing for diverse other human endeavours, 'astrological elections for sexual relations'. Apparently, 'the ideal time was when the moon was in Sagittarius.'[104] It is assumed that such elections were expected to help maximise one's chances of conceiving a healthy child rather than being astrological aphrodisiacs – the phrase commonly used in the almanacs, arguably evoking more of a sense of duty than of romance, is the somewhat prim 'be as a husband to thy wife'.[105]

In the tradition of the dog days, and other "unlucky day" traditions like it, we see the investment or incorporation of meaning into a set of dates. Certain days are afforded greater consequence or even specific distinction – relating a particular activity to a point in the annual calendar, thereby

---

104   Ibid, p. 121.

105   Gregory Burton, *Almanacke* (London, 1613), sig. B2v; see also William Dade, *Almanack* (London, 1647), sig. C4.

mapping and providing context for the annual cycle of the year. Most almanacs tabulated the 'common notes and moo[v]able Feasts' that punctuated the year.[106] This was especially true for rural life, where the rhythms of nature were paid particular attention. Along with providing a scale of meaning that divided up the year into activities – while also linking year-long cycles with the larger cosmic scales of planetary revolution and universal destiny – doctrines of unlucky days also once again demonstrated a combination of knowledge and action. By recognising these particularly significant days, especially the misfortunate ones, a preventative form of action took place.

CATASTROPHE

The use of astrology to predict natural disaster was long-established by the seventeenth century. Christopher Heydon points out that Christ 'forewarned the Jews to lift up their heads to heaven and to behold the signs that should be in the sun, and in the moon, and in the stars before [the fall of Jerusalem].'[107] However we should remember when discussing early modern "natural disasters" that humanity itself was considered part of the natural world. There was no sense of separation in astrology between great political, religious or otherwise human upheavals and floods, fires, tornados and other catastrophes. Astrology's universal scale of meaning considered all upheavals.

Astrology made prediction about such catastrophes as contemporary disaster warning, and also predicted the public mood itself. Astrologers helped construct the social meaning

---

106 Daniel Browne, *A New Almanacke* (London, 1620), p. 4.

107 C. Heydon, MS Ashmole 242, f. 63v; cf. Matthew xxiv: 29. Cited in Capp, *Astrology*, p. 134.

of naturally occurring events such as comets and eclipses. Some of the best examples of this type of effect are the events leading up to and surrounding the solar eclipse of March 1652. The agitation over this particular celestial phenomenon was considerable – consideration of the effect and meaning of this eclipse accounted for over a quarter of the March publications amassed by bookseller and collector George Thomason (1602-1666).[108] The reaction seems to have been one of widespread bewilderment and even outright terror at this 'Preamble of Doomsday'.[109] John Evelyn commented that, following predictions made by at least one contemporary astrologer regarding this solar eclipse, 'many were so terrified by [William] Lilly that they durst not go out of their houses.'[110] Thomas describes a truly apocalyptic scenario, with wealthy Londoners desperately fleeing the city, as the poor were left to scrabble for tonics[111] to counteract the effects of this dreadful event.[112] Capp constructs from evidence a similarly bleak report: 'other accounts speak of deserted streets and abandoned markets, and even of breakdowns and suicides.'[113] The effects of prophecies about catastrophes were not limited to creating mere general panic. As events could be influenced by prior human knowledge they might well take on a certain

---

108 Thomas, p. 354-5; cites *Catalogue of the Pamphlets... collected by George Thomason, 1640-61*, ed. G.K. Fortescue (London, 1908), I, p. 863-6.

109 Anon, *On Bugbear Black Monday* (1652).

110 Cited in Curry, p. 30.

111 The pamphlet claims that in fear of the eclipse's effect some drank 'Saffron'd Wine... and hide from Air...' We should notice from these cordials how knowledge of what was astrologically occurring was once again being turned to the manufacture and validation of techniques for actually affecting such influences.

112 Thomas, p. 355.

113 Capp, *Astrology*, p. 80.

self-fulfilling character. Indeed, 'contemporaries realized that...
prophecies [of famine in this case] could be self-fulfilling,
as farmers hoarded supplies and waited for prices to rise.'[114]
Likewise, from a contemporary (and critical) view, the charge
was levelled firmly against astrologers and their supporters as
being primary instigators of panic through their 'unknown
Characters of's horrid Pen' that purported to reveal the
'secrets of the Stars': one pamphlet raged, 'your foolish fears in
part were causes, why / The Women tremble, and the Children
cry'.[115] Clearly the power of astrology to interpret events in
the early modern environment was not always considered
matched with astrologers' sense of responsibility for those
interpretations. The position of astrologers as messengers of
the stars was fraught with the dangers of bearing bad news.

A fusing of magic and astrology occurs in the tirade of
the pamphlet mentioned above. Astrological symbols are
derided as esoteric and obtuse. The astrologer is accused of
'Conj'ring' and is referred to as a 'Magician' and a 'Wizard' who
'in their Black Art beguile[s]' – even as a 'frantick Prophet'.[116]
The pamphlet demonstrates a clear understanding of the
overlapping grounds and roles between astrologers, religious
figures and magicians. While this diatribe may demonstrate
a seventeenth-century dissatisfaction with occult arts such
as astrology, and with magic and the occult in general, the
conflation of magic and astrology should also illustrate that
there was a genuine cross-fertilisation of astrology and magic

---

114   Ibid, p. 64. Capp further notes that 'Henry Rogeford suppressed
details of the coming harvest to frustrate hoarders and prevent the
'impoverishment of the poor common people ': 'through my pen I
should not be the occasion of their malice' – citing Henry Rogeford,
Alwanacke [sic], (London, 1560), sig. B4.

115   Anon, *On Bugbear Black Monday* (1652).

116   Ibid.

in the early modern period. This pamphlet, after all, does offer insight into the precise mechanisms of astrology – for example, it accurately identifies and laments the universal scale of astrological analysis.[117] This was not a "rationalistic" anti-magical outcry against "superstitious" practices. It was a religious call to abandon fearful and socially disruptive eclipse-lore and to accept that 'God is the Guide, His Son, our Way, our Light'.[118] The astrologer, like the priest, attempted to act as a middleman or interpreter for the underlying foundations of existence. The clear difference between the two roles, that of astrologers' attempts to manage and manipulate such celestial influences, is perhaps the clearest indication of the fusing of astrologer and magician. It is for this reason, for the impertinence of attempting to become a director of divine power, that this pamphlet, in my opinion accurately, conflates magic and astrology.

The emphasis given here to the upheaval of this feared event is certainly not meant to highlight the gullibility of early modern people, but to illustrate that astrology played a vital role in the general tensions of millenarianism in the seventeenth century about a '*Sodome*-vengeance'.[119] These kinds of astrological scares demonstrate a disruptive and potentially dangerous dimension to astrology. Apparent foreknowledge of events affected the actions of participants forewarned of astrological forces. It therefore affected the outcome of an event, particularly in the case of tumult following fearful predictions. In particular, 'the furore over the solar eclipse of 29 March

---

117   'That every Action must pass your Scale / No Marriage, Bargaine, Journey, Physick, Fact / But Stars in every Scene are drest to Act.' Ibid.

118   Ibid.

119   Ibid.

1652, known as "Black Monday", revealed the potency of a combination of astrology and apocalypse."[120] Clearly these kinds of astrological predictions played a role in political considerations. In short, natural astrology did more than offer good planting times and weather forecasts – it provided disaster warnings and answers to the hows and whys of mass events. At the very least, it provided a language for analysis of these mass phenomena. By attempting to grant meaning to mass events from their timing and relation to the stars, astrology often encountered malevolent confluences of astral forces at the crux of a coming celestial event. In the mind of the astrologer, he was doubtlessly merely warning the public of an impending disaster. Yet the furore over Black Monday offers a glimpse at the extent of early modern comprehension that the astrologer was as much a subjective interpreter of the signs of the cosmos as an objective reporter. Indeed, 'no real objectivity could – or can – exist in deciphering God's providence'.[121] The pamphlet discussed above seems to be most incensed over this assumed authority and objectivity of the astrologers. The pamphlet perceives an astrological challenge to the 'common sense' objective truth of God and His works, and to the scare-mongering of suggesting that God would abandon those who did not indulge in magical protection.

ELECTION

By using 'Elections we may Governe, Order and Produce things as we please: *Faber quisq; Fortunæ propriæ*

---

120   Capp, *Astrology*, p. 79.

121   Ibid, p. 59.

[sic]'[122] This is how Ashmole extolled the great virtues of the practice of electing astrologically favourable times to begin a project. By understanding at what times the forces of the universe were well-disposed to support a particular kind of activity practitioners of astrology could take full advantage of such forces. The magus and court astrologer John Dee (1527-1609), was 'entrusted to choose the astrologically best fitting day for the coronation [of Elizabeth I (1533-1603)] in 1558.'[123] This illustrates the high regard in which elections were held and (although it arguably marks an Elizabethan zenith in the appraisal of election astrology) the practice remained a ubiquitious tool in the arsenal of the practicing astrologer well after the seventeenth century. Astrologers could elect a time for any conceivable question phrased "when should I do *x*?" Samuel Jeake, for example, seems to have used astrological means to decide when exactly to propose to the future Mrs Jeake, Elizabeth Hartshorne.[124] Ashmole frequently elected a time to make a journey. After setting one for a journey from London to Bradfield on the 27th December 1651, he reported 'a journey of great pleasure and good reception from friends.'[125] Elections not only ensured fate was not against your actions, but could maximise the success of the venture.

A common topic of election included timings for the laying of foundation stones of buildings. Vaughan Hart

---

122 Elias Ashmole, *Theatrum Chemicum Britannicum* (London, 1652), p. 451. The Latin phrase – which might 'every man is the architect of his own fortune' – is attributed to the Roman patrician Appius Claudius Caecus.

123 György E. Szőnyi, 'John Dee and Early Modern Occult Philosophy', *Literature Compass* 1 (2004), 1, p. 2.

124 Hunter and Gregory, p. 19.

125 Josten, p. 597.

describes how 'by tradition foundation ceremonies were performed at specific times calculated by astrology in an attempt to draw down favourable influence on the building work', and quotes one contemporary observing of building location regulations, that 'Some doe seem a little Astrological'.[126] Jeake elected a time for the building of his new storehouse, and Hunter and Gregory observe that he even had this figure 'let into the wall of the building like a kind of talisman.'[127] The truly talismanic nature of such an engraving should be considered in the context of image magic and the principle of sympathy. As astrological glyphs were thought to attract the power of thing they represented, an election figure adorning the project for which it was cast becomes as much of a magnet for the forces it depicts as a mere research exercise. Elections thereby demonstrate the interlinked nature of astrological knowledge and action applications, and also highlight how astrology's rationality cannot be clearly cut away from its magic. Just as knowledge and action are demonstrably fused in knowing when best to act, so too are astrology and magic a co-dependent admixture of symbol and utility. In election, the casting of a figure becomes more than measuring, even more than interpretation – it becomes a ritual in which certain times for action become sacralised, emphasised as they are underlined with astrological significance.

The practice of election demonstrates how astrological activity cannot be discretely divided between the proto-scientific knowledge systems utilised in divination, and those more overtly magical activities (such as talisman

---

126   Vaughan Hart, *Art and Magic in the Court of the Stuarts* (London, 1994), p. 107; citing H. Wotton, *The Elements of Architecture* (London, 1624), p. 3.

127   Hunter and Gregory, p. 13.

construction) which were designed to have an effect on the world. Elections were divinatory, in that astrological symbolism was interpreted to discern information, but such information consisted of instructions for how to favourably affect a venture – knowing *was* acting. Jeake's storehouse election and talismanic engraving further complicates scholarly attempts to divide astrology between practices to gain knowledge and practices to affect things. Jeake's astrological thinking can be located 'partly in assessing the broad circumstances in which he came to important decisions and partly in choosing exact moments at which to execute his plans.'[128] Jeake, like other astrological practitioners, not only used astrology for gaining knowledge of the world, but also for acting in it. Here I believe we glimpse the ways in which relatively widespread astrological divinatory knowledge systems, which could be explored within a rational natural law-like determinism, could also quickly stray into the more ritualised ceremonies of effects-centred enchantment magic. Elections, by their very nature, were a practice of imparting the express knowledge of how to affect a desired outcome. They represent how an astrological understanding of events also presented an opportunity to manage and manipulate such events prior to their occurrence. Such manipulation of events yet again illustrates how temporal context and human significance were closely united in a grand universal system of astrological meaning. People did not have to be at the mercy of vast impersonal forces – astrological election offered a chance to utilise the ebb and flow of cosmic assistances and hindrances for one's own benefit. Elections allowed early modern astrologers and their audience to be active and responsible participants in an unfolding of destiny.

---

128   Hunter and Gregory, p. 74.

Such an analysis is not merely the benefit of hindsight – early modern contemporaries were similarly aware of the grey area into which elections fell between legitimate Christian natural philosophy and powerful, even potentially questionable, sorcery. Such awareness is demonstrated by Jeake's unease and defensiveness around the topic of elections, even in his own diary. Jeake makes an election but hides his confession of it in shorthand. Elsewhere Jeake repeatedly and somewhat defensively denies making elections over activities typically elected for, such as making a long journey.[129] The fusing of magic and astrology, demonstrated in election, was clearly something understood by early modern practitioners. Election was more than forecasting, it was enchanting.

As has already been suggested in the discussion of astrology and agriculture, the most advantageous times to harvest plants and herbs in order to utilise their 'occult virtues' to maximum effect were also governed by astrological considerations. Ingredients for medicinal or other magical usages were astrologically encoded with layers of meaning and effect, directly dependent upon the time they were collected for use. These astrological harvest timings were derived from the stars that were thought to rule the plant or herb in question. Speaking of the herb angelica astrologer-physician Nicholas Culpeper (1616-1654) advises 'It is an herb of the Sun in Leo; let it be gathered when he [the Sun] is there [Leo], and the Moon applying to his good Aspect; let it be gathered either in his hour, or in the hour of Jupiter [a planet 'friendly' to the Sun[130]]... Observe the like in gathering the herbs of other Plants, and

---

129   Ibid, p. 13, 56, 230, 235.

130   Lilly, *Christian Astrology*, p. 65, 72.

you may happen [to] do wonders.'[131] Astrology once more linked natural phenomena, such as the growth of flora, to the processes of time and destiny. Election furthermore underlined particular periods during which a plant or herb was considered especially significant, as astrology combined a universal and interlinking system of meaning with notions of occult virtue.

ENVIRONMENTAL CONCLUSIONS

In the current scholarship of astrology, "natural astrology" has often been defined as dealing with this 'natural law-like determinism' that linked it to approaches of natural philosophy. Yet this definition implicitly requires a distinction to be drawn between astrologies of nature and of magic, between the natural and the supernatural, that does not seem to be justified by the majority of early modern astrological activity. It may be tempting for the modern secular materialist to consider nature the very opposite of magic: one is evidently the measurable reality of the cosmos and can be subjected to rigorous empirical testing, the other is essentially defined (in much modern parlance) as anything outside of the authority of physics, that which is relegated to the freakish, the non-normal, the unexplainable, even the fallacious or merely pseudo-scientific. This non-natural definition of magic, and even to some extent, this non-magical conception of nature, would be very alien to early modern thinkers.

That is not to say that the term 'supernatural' itself was not used at all in the early modern period. But it should certainly be noted that the word has very different meanings from the modern usages. It is, for example, used at one point

---

131   Nicholas Culpeper, *The English Physician* (London, 1652), p. 8.

in Agrippa's *Three Books* to explain the magical principles of reflection and sympathy:

'For this is the harmony of the world, that things supercelestiall be drawn down by the Celestiall, and the super-naturall by naturall, *because there is one operative vertue that is diffused through all kinds of things, by which vertue indeed, as manifest things are produced out of occult causes...*'[132]

The supernatural is considered merely the superlunary influence drawn by the natural. Moreover Agrippa suggests that, while these things are located in different tiers of the Neoplatonic cosmic hierarchy known as the Great Chain of Being, they are of the same essential force. A natural thing must possess its particular occult properties, essences or 'vertues', responsible for its form and function. This is the unity of manifest things in this world; that all of nature operates by such 'vertues'. This is clearly not a use of 'supernatural' to support or encourage a separation between natural and magical, and certainly not a bifurcation of early modern knowledge into exclusive categories of rational empiricism and non-rational magic. The 'one operative vertue' is a description of the organisation and operation of a holistic magical universe.[133]

For astrologers, 'nature was infused with divinity, spirituality and magicality'.[134] Patrick Curry, speaking of both astrologer-herbalist Nicholas Culpeper and the

---

132   Agrippa, *Three Books*, I, Ch 38

133   For more on natural magic and the term 'supernatural', see John Henry, 'The Fragmentation of Renaissance Occultism and the Decline of Magic', *History of Science*, 46, I, 151 (March 2008).

134   Curry, *Prophecy and Power*, p. 24.

alchemist and physician known as Paracelsus,[135] sums up this
attitude as a 'naturalism-cum-supernaturalism'.[136] Astrology
operated in a natural *and* magical world. In the 1658 English
translation of his *Natural Magick*, Giambattista della Porta
(c. 1535-1615) – Anglicised to John Baptista Porta – explains
the natural basis of this magic with particular reference to
the advantages to be gained from studying the stars:

> '...I think that Magick is nothing else but the
> survey of the whole course of Nature. For, whilst
> we consider the Heavens, the Stars, the Elements,
> how they are moved, and how they are changed,
> by this means we find out the hidden secrecies of
> living creatures, of plants, of metals, and of their
> generation and corruption...'[137]

It is these 'hidden secrecies' we should bear in mind when
considering early modern occult philosophy. The "occluded"
element of magical practice seems less about veiled elite
knowledge than simply pursuit of the hidden inner workings
of life. Bearing in mind that metals were commonly regarded as
organic, and thought to grow in the veins of the earth, Porta's
wider point seems clear. Each of the forms of life – animals,
plants, metals – existed and functioned (literally) by *virtue* of
their 'hidden secrecies'. Such study of the occult virtues of
things 'openeth unto us the properties and qualities of hidden
things, and the knowledge of the whole course of Nature...'[138]

---

135   Philippus Aureolus Theophrastus Bombastus von Hohenheim (1493-
      1541)

136   Curry, p. 24.

137   Jean Baptista Porta, *Natural Magick* (London, 1658), p. 2

138   Porta, *Natural Magick*, p. 2

By comprehending the forces influencing one form of the life of the cosmos, one could get at principles that could be used to understand another form. This thoroughly rational conclusion was arrived at from magical premises such as the principle of reflection: the laws of the macrocosmic stars could be applied to the microcosmically human scale – to empires and even individual patients. Thus a doctor of astrology could be a physicist, an economist and a physician. Astrology used rational analysis to carry out magical activities – whether that was drawing influence into an object to act as a "fate-magnet" that would draw the desired change to us, or in manipulating the outcome of events by making judgements and actions based upon knowledge of occult properties and operations.

We have seen in this chapter how magical tonics were sold against putrefactions expected as a result of an eclipse; how agricultural elections attempted to ensure the best crop by knowing about the magical ways nature worked; and, finally, how amulets were used to affect nature directly. Along with providing illustrations of what natural magic looked like, we can draw a further significance from considering these examples of action in an early modern magical cosmos: that knowledge was a means to action, of ensuring a useful and beneficial outcome. The use of amulets is perhaps the most obvious form of this natural magical action, and one that deserves some further consideration.

Keith Thomas stated in 1971, 'the one widely practiced type of magic which rested on clearly stated astrological foundations was the construction of astrological sigils and talismans, in which appropriate heavenly influences were caught like fruit as they fell and stored up for use when needed.'[139] While I contend that many other widely

---

139   Thomas, p. 759

practiced forms of magic also depended on astrological principles, I thoroughly agree that the construction of sigils is perhaps the clearest link between magic and astrology, and also the clearest example of the use of knowledge of magical nature to affect the world to one's advantage. The streaming forces of the stars pulsed and fluxed in accordance with God's design, and attempts to collect such influences into suitably-marked containers were no more inherently unnatural or irrational than bringing in a crop at harvest-time. Nature appointed a time at which nourishment would sprout from the earth and fall from the skies. A canny operator could catch the fruits of the stars just as they would pick the blooms of medicinal plants at the proper time of their blossoming.

Significantly, this consideration of the construction of astrological sigils as storing fruit is not one that escaped early modern thinkers. Porta remarks of exactly such processes that, 'as in Husbandry, it is Nature that bring forth corn and herbs, but it is Art that prepares and makes way for them.'[140] Such a comment highlights the importance of the artful craft of the magical operator, while also maintaining Porta's characterisation of Magick as the 'handmaid' of Nature. We do not hold dominion over the stars, any more than we can command rivers, but we can make best preparation for their flow and even harness their force for our mills.

As a final comment, the totality of early modern nature's domain should also be emphasised. Magical astrological virtue and correspondence existed in all creation and in all processes. Astrology traced the lattices and knot-works of this web of correspondences, and astrologers picked harmonies from the strung threads of an interconnected universe.

---

140   Porta, *Natural Magick*, p. 2.

The symbolism of magic and astrology contributed significantly to human knowledge. The sevenfold taxonomy of planetary characteristics was used to understand many processes. Lilly's angelic periodisation explains history as the efforts and effects of people under particular celestial influence. It gives reasons *why* people acted as they did. It provided a basis for analysis of action. Astrology explored underlying forces to produce knowledge, which would affect action. From astrological considerations of the cyclicality of nature, predictive analytical activity (and not merely hindsighted explanation) could take place. There was certainly a sense of "cosmological security" in having faith in nature's predictability. Yet more than security, the prospect of foreknowledge allowed analysis to look forward, to better one's chances. Awareness of vast forces allowed the self-direction of efforts. Far from constructing a system of scapegoating the stars, I believe astrological activity could encourage a responsibility for one's actions, or at least an understanding that such actions did not occur in an environmental vacuum. Astrologers were analytical "liminaries"[141] existing on the threshold between people and their environmental context. Like the clergy, they acted as mediators between an underlying divine plan and the living of everyday life. Astrologers were a kind of magician, natural philosopher and speculative theoretician combined; exploring with great ingenuity and imagination the utility of their knowledge.

Astrology dealt with knowledge of the underlying destiny of time and the natural world. Environment was not merely what surrounds us, not merely a location for human endeavour. Environment was a process and a unity.

---

141 This term is taken from John Middleton, 'Spirit Possession among the Lugbara', in *Spirit Mediumship and Society in Africa*, ed. J. Beattie and J. Middleton (London, 1969), p. 220-31.

Nature was more than a static resource to be used; it was a total weave and weft of dynamic and interrelating rhythms of interaction. Astrological factors were similarly fluid influences. The waxing and waning of astral influences were in constant flux, as planets revolved into and out of particular signs and configurations.

Astrology united all natural phenomena by common analysis. The quotidian and small was linked all the way up to the cosmically big. Indeed, it is this 'comprehensiveness' that Thomas remarks 'made the art so compelling.'[142] Astrology located human activity within a universal scale of meaning. Human activity became an expression *of* the universe, not merely an alienated agency acting in or upon it. Astrology made human action and experience part of the natural world. In this way, astrology fostered a unique connection between people and environment.

So astrology built and maintained conceptual bridges between identity and environment. This was not simply a matter of "nature vs. nurture". Astrology did more than present an initial nativity of astrological factors governing a person's life based on birth. It accounted for fluctuations in a vast host of affecting influences throughout human experience. Astrology sought to locate all human acts (birth, sex, death and what happened in-between) within a context of influencing factors.[143] We could not, astrologically speaking, operate in a vacuum – no area of life was exempt from astrological analysis. It was in this manner that astrologers operated as interpreters of the environment, communicating the significances of nature. Consideration of nature was a matter of observation, measurement and speculation, very like such contributions made by astronomy and natural

---

142   Thomas, p. 384.

143   For more of these types of functions, see Chapter 4.

philosophy. Futhermore however, the symbols, conventions and assumption-structures of astrology and occultism also contributed to understanding the significances and human meaning of nature.

CHAPTER 3
THE POLITICAL

AS HAS BEEN DEMONSTRATED, ASTROLOGY EXTENDED
analysis into all areas of human life: all events, tendencies,
and eventualities could be investigated in the heavens.
Historian of astrology Ann Geneva makes a striking
analogy: 'Like economists, astrologers rarely made correct
predictions; yet universities granted degrees in the subject
and few heads of state made a move without them.'[144]
It is this prestigious economist-like role that astrologers
fulfilled with both judicial and horary astrology – that
is, making particular speculations and predictions about
human events, either on a broad national political scale
(the judicial) or a more detailed level of personal and
individual problems or concerns (the horary). Astrology
provided an analytical system that could address the
totality of human experience. Economics was certainly
one of the contexts of early modern living that astrology
touched upon, most often through a combination of these
wider political judgements and personal consultancy that
made up the workload of astrological practitioners. Yet
the coming of the civil war prompted a resurgence of
specifically political astrological speculation.[145] After 1640
political prognostication certainly became more specific,

---

144   Geneva, p. xv-xvi.

145   For more on the wider context of the Civil War, see John Morrill
        (ed.), *The Impact of the Civil War* (London, 1991).

widespread and commonplace.[146] The political application of astrological prophecy even continued throughout the later Restoration Crisis.[147]

George Wharton offers us the most common kind of argument that justified astrology as useful for political analysis:

> '*Heaven*...most effectually operates upon a Humane Body... and so also on the Body both of the Prince himself and his subjects ; to wit, so, as that it changes the Temperaments of Mens Bodies, and with those Temperaments their manners or conditions: and the manners or conditions of Princes and Subjects being changed, a Mutation of the Common-wealth followeth.'[148]

Astrology offered a way to comprehend how political developments emerged from changing human predispositions, especially those of autocratic leaders. Small wonder that 'until nearly the end of the [seventeenth] century it remained conventional for most political issues to be given some form of astrological expression.'[149] Astrology offered understanding of political affairs through assessments of relationships between individuals and nature. It was the grand aspiration of astrology to explore, as a unity, what has since been separated in modern assessments into natural philosophy and magic: to unite people and their environment, and the governing

---

146   Capp, *Astrology*, p. 35.

147   See W.E. Burns, 'A Whig Apocalypse: Astrology, Millenarianism, and Politics in England During the Restoration Crisis, 1678-1683', in J.E Force and R.H. Popkin (eds.), *Millenarianism and Messianism in Early Modern European Culture: The Millenarian Turn* (London, 2001), p. 29-41.

148   Wharton, *Hemeroscopeion Anni aerae*, p. 34-5.

149   Thomas, p. 407.

of humans and the wider universe, with a set of universally applicable frameworks. It was these aspirations that allowed the formulation of an astrological language for understanding politics to be so widely and usefully utilised.

The term "judicial" is sometimes also used to refer to any astrological activities (such as horary work) that did not fall into the category of "natural astrology".[150] However as we have seen, natural astrology viewed the affairs of humans, along with their technology and culture, as equally as natural as unspoilt wild environments. Both forms of astrology have a political dimension. "Judicial" as a general term for divinatory astrology is not a useful taxon, particularly if applied to astrological elections. Nevertheless, judicial astrology can be considered a unique type of astrological activity – that of making judgements on particular national political events. This definition of judicial astrology distinguishes it from the personal consultancy of horary and nativity astrology although, as we shall see, these two techniques were also used for expressly political purposes. One might be tempted to draw a distinction between astrological judgements on socio-political events based on human knowledge and reason, and the prophetic judicial astrological appeals to God and magic – Ashmole does consider 'Iudicall Astrologie... the Key of Naturall Magick, and Natural Magick the Doore that leads to this Blessed [Philosopher's] Stone.'[151] Yet the actual methods and practicalities of these supposedly different forms – of casting figures, interpreting their symbolisms, and extrapolating projections – are all too similar.

---

150   'It was a medieval and early modern commonplace that, broadly speaking, there were two kinds of astrology: natural and judicial'. Curry, p. 8.

151   Ashmole, *Theatrum Chemicum Britannicum*, p. 443; cited in Josten, 468-9.

PROPHECY

Prophecy was a central part of the judicial astrologers' craft. After all, 'in the experience of most people, politics, religion and eschatology were ultimately inseparable; and astrological prophecy was a common thread through all.'[152] The use of prophecy demonstrates the status and expertise afforded to astrologers as analysts of future events. Astrologers interpreted the symbolic language of prophecies into messages relating to contemporary affairs. In *Monarchy or No Monarchy*, Lilly prints 'Grebner's Prophecy of our late King and his sonne now King' in Latin, and then literally translates it. Moreover, he provides a detailed analysis of these symbols following the translations, in particular the 'Lyon of the North'.[153] Lilly even goes on later to equate this 'Lyon' with the sign Leo, and therefore with King Charles.[154] As a more general observation, it might help understanding of the political role of an astrologer to note that a 1626 English dictionary has the rather concise definition for "Astrologie" as 'A foretelling of things to come'.[155] There is no specific mention of stars. Astrologers could be forecasters of all things, a role certainly linked with astrology's universal scope.

The importance of prophecy in early modern English rebellions was both great and widely accepted.[156] When Rusche paraphrases Rupert Taylor's *The Political Prophecy in England* as emphasising the cross-class appeal of political

---

152   Curry, p. 22.

153   William Lilly, *Monarchy or No Monarchy* (London, 1651), p. 11-20.

154   Lilly, *Monarchy or No Monarchy*, p. 56.

155   Henry Cockeram, *The English dictionarie* (London, 1626).

156   Capp, *Astrology and the Popular Press*, p. 69; citing Thomas, *Religion* chapter 13.

prophecy, he claims prophecies were well circulated by a variety of sorts of people who 'at times even acted upon them.'[157] These prophetic efforts were popular – it is claimed of Lilly's version of the *White King* prophecy that '1,800 copies were sold in three days, and it was often reprinted during the next few years.'[158] Rusche is cautious not to draw 'definite relationships of cause and effect between particular prophecies and specific historical events', yet he nevertheless affirms that 'prophecies were given so much attention during the civil wars that one can safely conclude that they were a factor in the political affairs of the period.'[159] Millenarian concerns, which combined astrology and eschatology with political analysis, were an important factor – 'it has been estimated some seventy-percent of the ministers supporting Parliament saw the conflict in millennial terms'.[160] Astrologers such as Christopher Ness also presented 'astrological and eschatological wonders firmly into the context of current English political events'

---

157   Harry Rusche, 'Prophecies and Propaganda, 1641 to 1651', in *The English Historical Review*, 84, No. 333 (October, 1969), p. 752.

158   Harry Rusche, 'Merlini Anglici: Astrology and Propaganda from 1644 to 1651', *English Historical Review,* 80 (1965), p. 324 n 1. Thomas notes this information 'cannot be checked, but the accidental survival of a printer's bill reveals that the *Collection of Ancient and Moderne Prophecies* (1645) went into three impressions, representing a total of 4,500 copies' – Thomas, p. 489, citing H.R Plower, 'A printer's Bill in the Seventeenth Century', *The Library*, new ser., vii (1906).

159   Rusche, 'Prophecies and Propaganda', p. 753.

160   J. Wojcik, 'Robert Boyle, The Conversion of the Jews, and Millenial Expectations', in J.E. Force and R.H. Popkin (eds.), *Millenarianism and Messianism in Early Modern European Culture: The Millenarian Turn* (Dordrecht, 2001), p. 55; citing Capp, *Fifth Monarchy Men*, pp. 38, 41. Wojcik points out 'Many royalists, too, saw the war in these terms although, apparently, millennial expectations were not quite so widespread on that side.' Ibid.

during the Restoration Crisis.[161] The political dimensions of prophecy are clear in the work of seventeenth-century judicial astrologers. Astrologers were occult interpreters, describing the shape of the future, and their audience was fascinated by their interpretations.

As well as penning their own forecasts, many astrologers were in the habit of adopting older and established prophecies and giving them new contemporary interpretations. The works of Mother Shipton provided particularly good utility to the parliamentary cause for example, as she predicted that, following a violent conflict, 'there shall never be warfare againe, nor any more Kings or Queenes'.[162] Lilly includes one of Shipton's forecasts in an annotated summary of 'severall ancient English Prophecies, affirming there shall be no more Kings in England' in his *Monarchy or No Monarchy* of 1651.[163]

Another example of astrologers recycling prophecy is Lilly's use of the long-extant *Prophecy of the White King*[164] to make dire warnings about the eventual downfall of King Charles I (1600-1649). By 1651 Lilly claimed that '*Charls* late deceased... was without dispute the true White King.'[165] In 1644 Lilly combined this and a further prophecy known as *The Dreadful Dead-man*, taken from John Harvey's *A Discoursive Probleme concerning Prophecies* (London, 1588)[166] to claim that 'Monarchy shall be eclipsed and darkened', itself a

---

161 Burns, 'A Whig Apocalypse', p. 34.

162 Mother Shipton, *Mercurius propheticus or a collection of some old predictions* (London, 1644), p. 6.

163 Lilly, *Monarchy or No Monarchy*, p. 55-66.

164 Rusche, 'Prophecy and Propaganda', p. 757; citing Rupert Taylor, *The Political Prophecy in England* (New York, 1911), p. 21-23, 103.

165 William Lilly, *Merlinin Anglici ephemeris* (London, 1651), sig A2v.

166 Rusche, 'Prophecy and Propaganda', p. 759.

phrasing not without portentous astrological significance.[167]
Rusche seems certain that this identification of Charles with
"the White King" would have been obvious to seventeenth-
century readers, who would have been well aware that this
identification would spell trouble for the king. Rusche even
offers accounts of the Earl of Pembroke attempting to
persuade Charles to wear the traditional purple coronation
robes by citing 'the violent deaths of Richard II and Henry
VI, the two monarchs who had previously broken with
tradition to wear white at their coronations.'[168]

Speculation on future events by astrologers was not
limited to figures that they themselves cast. Astrologers'
primary role was to forecast the future by interpreting
symbolism – whether that be the signs in the stars or the
predictions of ancient prophecy. Indeed, it has been pointed
out that many prophecies chiefly,

> 'drew their prestige from their antiquity, and that
> although some contemporaries discussed whether
> the prophets had got their foreknowledge from
> God, from conjuration or from astrology, there was
> on the whole little interest shown in the precise
> origin and basis of such predictions. For most men
> it was sufficient that they were there.'[169]

This assessment not only illustrates an early modern
prioritisation of the *use* of prophecy over assessment of

---

167 William Lilly, *A Prophecy of the White King and Dreadfull Dead-man
    Explaned* (London, 1644), p. 4.

168 Rusche, 'Prophecy and Propaganda', p. 757; citing 'two unsigned
    articles, one in *Quarterly Review*, xxvi (1822) 192, the other in *Notes
    and Queries*, ii (1862), 351.'

169 Thomas, p. 469.

fundamental truth value, it also demonstrates how astrology was co-mingled in popular conceptions with magic, and indeed religiosity and spirituality, as a means of synthesising spontaneous knowledge.

When discussing overlap between religion and astrology, particularly in the context of prophecy, we should also include use of the Bible by astrologers. We have already discussed John Booker's *The Bloody Almanack*, described by Rachum as 'a pro-parliament presentation of John Napier's 1593 study of Revelation'[170] which attempted to synthesise astrological proofs of historical crises with symbolism in Revelation to create both a periodisation of Christian history and a projected date for the end of the world. It is certainly a drastic condensing of the some 280-page tome of John Napier (1550-1617) into an eminently more accessible 6-page almanac. Revelation, 'always a rich source of astrological symbolism',[171] was also used by the minister Edmund Reeve (d. 1660) in his sermon *The New Jerusalem* delivered to the Society of Astrologers at their feast on 8th August 1650.[172] Another Scriptural sermon delivered 1st August 1649 at the Astrologers' Feasts was *A New Starre Leading Wisemen unto Christ* by clergyman Robert Gell (1595-1665) – as can be deduced from the title, this sermon discussed the 'Star in the East' which had led the Magi to the Christ-child.[173]

---

170   Rachum, 'The Term 'Revolution'', p. 871. For more on Booker's *Bloody Almanack* and astrology's relationship with Scriptural prophecy see Chapter 2.

171   Curry, p. 42.

172   *Dictionary of National Biography*, XVI, p. 848-49; cited in Curry, p. 42 n 82. For more on the Society's feasts, see Curry, p. 40-44.

173   From Matthew 2:2. Robert Gell, *Stella Nova, A new starre leading wisemen unto Christ* (London, 1649), p. 1.

Astrologers of the Christian early modern period were understandably fond of using accounts of prophecy from the Bible involving celestial events to argue for the legitimacy and authority of their craft. Without entering into extended coverage of attacks and defences of astrology in this period, it is pertinent to note that the Bible has been described as 'unfortunately... ambiguous' on astrology's legitimacy.[174] A favourite passage for astrologers was Genesis 1:14,[175] which was used as a basis for a sermon by Roman Catholic priest Richard Carpenter (1604/5-1670?).[176] It is Carpenter's considered opinion that this passage should be read to say that 'the Stars and Planets are *Signs*: as *signifying* in their *motions, conjunctions, oppositions, risings, settings, occultations, apparitions, defections*, and *various Relations* and *Aspects* ; and as *acting* by their *influences*.'[177] He follows this interpretation with an etymological proof – 'Whence the *Hebrews* name the Stars, *Massaloth*, being a word bred and born of *Nazal, influere, to give* influx *or* influence.'[178] Regardless of the accuracy of this assessment, such a case highlights how astrologers not only interpreted the Bible, but even interpreted the Hebrew roots of its text. Prophecy reinterpretation by astrologers was demonstrably not to be limited to magical prophecy, nor to relatively contemporary divinely-inspired works, but included exegesis of established Biblical texts.

---

174   D.C. Allen, *The Star-Crossed Renaissance* (London, 1966), p. 48.

175   'And God said, Let there bee lights in the firmament of the heauen, to divide the day from the night : and let them bee for signes, and for seasons, and for dayes and yeeres.' *The Holy Bible* (London, 1619), sig A3.

176   Richard Carpenter, *Astrology Proved Harmless, Useful, Pious* (London, 1656).

177   Ibid, p. 3.

178   Ibid, p. 3-4.

Perhaps the most frequent reinterpretation of the astrology of others was in the refutations of judgements made by adversarial astrologers during the ongoing pamphlet propagandising around the civil wars.[179] This was expressly the opposite of citing respected older works to increase the recognised legitimacy of one's own prognostications. It was a battle of aggressive pop-academic one-upmanship, with the express purpose of both co-opting the astrological data used by rivals for one's own ends and, as was more often the case, rubbishing the credentials of said antagonists. The latter activity was far more common than the former, owing partly to common conventions of astrological symbolism – most obviously, the Sun as a symbol of royalty and governors. As such, it was far more common to emphasise a part of a figure one's rival astrologer had overlooked to arrive at an opposing viewpoint – and to undermine their political opinion. So, between 'royalist astrological symbolism', such as that of George Wharton, and Parliamentarian symbolism, such as William Lilly's, there were certainly different, even 'inverted', significances.[180] When interpreting a horary figure, set for the time of 'His Majesties present Martch: begun from Oxford May 7 1645', Wharton emphasises *inter alia* that 'the Regall signe Leo' is in the first house and that the Sun, Venus and Jupiter are in fortuitous positions. He insists that 'these are evident and undeniable Testimonies' of the king's success.[181] In contrast, Lilly claimed that the position of Mercury, 'simply the most strong in this present figure' (a fact that Wharton affirmed by 'his own words at this time') meant that the victory assured in the figure would

---

179   See section on propaganda, Chapter 3.

180   Geneva, p. 194.

181   George Wharton, *An Astrologicall Judgement Upon His Majesties Martch* (Oxford, 1645), sig B3.

go to that which was signified by a sign ruled by Mercury. In this case, 'Gemini is the ascendant of the City of London all Authors agree', and seeing as Mercury was 'Lord of that signe', Lilly interpreted the figure to mean that the 'City and Citizens' of London would be victorious 'by being the Kingdomes Bulwarke against Tyranny and Oppression.' He furthermore added that 'this city shall get into their power... all their enemies... for we see *Mercury* disposeth of *Jupiter*.'[182] Such examples reflect 'the remarkable flexibility of astrology as an interpretive language system'.[183] They also further emphasise the interpreter role of astrologers, especially those making expressly political judgments.

Historians of science have relished emphasising the examples of empirical correlation that astro-meteorology so neatly provides. As mentioned above, the weather logs of Jeake and others offer much to analyse.[184] However we should also remember that astrological meteorological analysis was used for expressly political purposes, in prophesising the fate of kings and kingdoms from natural portents. Geneva notes that the thoroughly political astrologer-prophet William Lilly made use of several different celestial phenomena in his pamphlets, many of which had 'long traditions of interpretive analysis within astrology: comets, eclipses, and the periodic conjunctions of... Saturn and Jupiter'.[185] Eclipses and their astrological coordinates were used to demonstrate the natures of political organisations. On 3rd November 1640, Elias Ashmole noted in his diary: 'At the first sitting of the Long Parliament the Sun was Eclipsed in 21 degr: of [Scorpio] and

---

182   Lilly, *The Starry Messenger* (London, 1645), postscript.

183   Geneva, p. 193.

184   For more on astrology and environment, see Chapter 2.

185   Geneva, p. 83.

their actions were sutable to the falce viperous & trecherous nature of that signe, swift & violent as lightning."[186] Celestial events occurring at the outset of a venture were particularly useful in assessing the nature and significance of that venture. By finding and analysing a 'sutable' symbol or analogy (such as the scorpion), astrological knowledge about the signified organisation could be explored, and a political assessment could be quickly reached. Such an assessment also linked the event to a specific point in time, affording it a unique role in the overall destiny of the universe.

The divinely-inspired or unveiled ancient wisdom of prophecy is based upon an often revelatory understanding of fundamental forces underlying existence. Astrology and prophecy frequently cross-pollinated each other – astrological symbolism was frequently used to interpret the 'wealth and polyvalence of prophetic language'.[187] Their most frequently shared ground was political assessment and speculation. The distinction between rational human projections about future events and divinely-inspired prophecy was not a clear one. Both explanations for their methodologies were used by astrologers in their predictions. Richard Napier reportedly summoned the archangel Raphael to give patient diagnoses, discuss theology and deliver prophecy.[188] The astrologer acted as a receiver and relay for communications from the forces underlying mundane reality. This is a somewhat definitional model of the function of a prophet. The active conjuration of

---

186   MS Ashm. 313, f. 10; cited in Josten, p. 331.

187   Ottavia Niccoli, *Prophecy and People in Renaissance Italy* (Princeton, 1990), p. 35.

188   See Michael MacDonald, *Mystical Bedlam : Madness, Anxiety and Healing in Seventeenth Century England* (Cambridge, 1981), pp. 210, 16, 18 respectively. See also the section on mind, body, and soul, Chapter 4.

angels or other sources of divine knowledge however (rather than being visited unexpectedly or unbidden), as performed by Napier and doubtlessly by other astrologer-magicians, presents a further complication. For astrologers, there was active engagement in seeking information and interpreting those answers into action.

For much of the early modern period leading up to the seventeenth century, astrologers had been able to couch their prognostications in the language of visionary theology as well as that of "scientific" prediction. Lilly has been described as an astrologer 'who could unselfconsciously... issue his predictions as prophecies.'[189] In the early modern period, religiosity in politics was generally considered a desirable if not downright necessary quality. We find then in political astrological activity the means to marry broad religious knowledge and values with particular political decision-making and action. This seventeenth-century attitude has been summed up as being of 'a time when natural, civil and religious phenomena were still widely seen as connected, if not indeed one'.[190] Astrology could offer a means to practical piety, taking heed of the stars that God had set in the heavens to act as 'signes' to guide us.

Astrologers publishing political judgements on existing magical prophecies, even phrasing their own political predictions in visionary voices, demonstrate how astrology was considered within a wider scope of religious and magical activity, which also included conjuration of angels or spirits and magical divination, as part of Christian spirituality and piety.[191] Astrology promoted the understanding of, and the

---

189 Curry, p. 31.

190 Ibid, p. 22.

191 See section on personal consultancy, Chapter 4..

operating within, a divinely-ordained magical natural world –
that early modern viewpoint characterised as 'naturalism-
cum-supernaturalism'. Political astrology operated in a
context that conflated intellectual, religious and magical
roles. Likewise, prophecy demonstrates how political wisdom
did not always come from claims of the objective truth-value
of statements, beliefs and actions, but often from practices
designed to best illustrate particular links between people
and the underlying divine order. Ottavia Niccoli, speaking
of sixteenth-century Italy, has observed that 'prophecy
seems to have constituted a unifying sign connecting nature
to religion and religion to politics and coordinating all the
scattered shreds of a culture that in the end turned out to
be an integral way of knowing embracing observation of
nature, political analysis, and religious reflection.'[192] I would
suggest not only that this insightful observation rings true
for the later English context of prophecy, but also for the
astrology that was used to analyse, interpret and disseminate
such prophecy. The political context of astrology emerged
from observing the influences that unite the microcosmic
individual with the wider macrocosmic universe.

ANALYSIS

Along with examples of words with obvious linguistic
foundations in astrological symbolism (e.g. "saturnine")
there are words in modern English usage that come directly
from astrological terminology. The roots of the term
"revolution" are astrological, and significant for considering
the political contexts of astrology and its efforts to combine
the individual with the cosmos. The word clearly originates
in astrological and astronomical language, meaning the

---

192   Niccoli, p. xvi.

completion of a cycle, referring originally to planetary motion. In 1626 therefore 'Reuolution' was defined as 'A winding or turning about, especially in the course of time.'[193] The intellectual cipher to unlocking the term's shift from a purely astronomical measurement of time to one that signified change in human events is certainly also astrological. As the planets completed their cycles, new astral influences permeated the world, and "revolution" could therefore be used to discuss a transformation or new direction of events. Rachum traces a particularly significant usage of the word to physician Thomas Browne (1605-1682), who, along with using it in a traditional temporal periodic sense to refer to the 'revolution of Saturn', wrote that 'the glory of one State depends upon the ruin of another, there is a revolution and vicissitude of their greatness, and must obey the swing of that wheel'.[194] The term revolution provides an example of the linguistic dimension of astrology's contribution to early modern politics in particular and culture in general.

Although the intellectual roots of this shift in meaning are undoubtedly astrological, Rachum expresses puzzlement at a general 'inability or unwillingness [of astrologers themselves] to employ "revolution" in a political sense', especially during the very period when this new use of the term was being popularised.[195] I would suggest that a lack of consideration of "revolution" as a specific technique of astrological activity in Rachum's essay may at least help to explain this apparent recalcitrance. "Revolution", as well as being a term for periods of planetary cycles and therefore

---

193   Cockeram, *The English dictionarie* (1626).

194   Rachum, 'The Term 'Revolution'', p. 871; citing *The Works of Sir Thomas Browne*, ed. C. Sayle, 3 vols (Edinburgh, 1912), I, pp. 13, 25, 28-9, 59.

195   Rachum, 'The Term 'Revolution'', p. 874 and passim.

change, also referred to an astrological practice whereby a new figure of the heavens was set for the precise moment the sun re-entered the position it occupied at the moment of a person's birth. The birth figure was "revolved" or spun forwards like a clock, until the Sun came back to the position it had occupied before the revolution had been made. This 'annual revolution' of a nativity figure, having shifted each of the stars around the chart, could then be interpreted to answer questions about the coming year – uniting the native with factors that would affect them. The revolution was both a personalised version of a horary chart and a modified type of nativity chart. It related the individual's particular astrological birth influences to the events in their life over a specific coming year. Ashmole records performing such a revolution in 1655.[196] His interpretation notes illustrate, as Josten points out, 'what fears and hopes occupied Ashmole's mind at the time'.[197] One such hope was for a 'reconciliation between the Native [i.e. Ashmole] & his wife' which, sadly, the revolution only demonstrated 'rather the Natives willignes to seeke it, th[a]n hopes of obteyning it'.[198] This annual revolution also provided the native with a type of astrological early warning system. Noting the appearance of '[Saturn] in [Virgo] in [quartile] to the Ascendant of the Radix', Ashmole judges that this will 'afflict the Native with Melancholly and may occasion some sicknes.'[199]

Such an example demonstrates that revolution was already a type of intellectual activity for astrologers. The term already had general descriptive values, of a period

---

196   MS Ashm. 430, ff 92-3v; cited in Josten, p. 674.

197   Josten, p. 674.

198   MS Ashm. 430, ff 92-3v; cited in Josten, p. 674.

199   MS Ashm. 430, ff 92-3v; cited in Josten, p. 675.

of time and of change – yet also had a specific technique and activity ascribed to it. I suggest then that this extant meaning or context of "revolution" as a thing that can be brought about *by* human activity, rather than a phenomenon that occurs *to* humans, may help explain why early modern astrologers themselves were not typically users of the word in its modern political meaning, despite the newer term's clear intellectual roots in astrology. The concept of participating in, instigating or *making* a revolution would already have a defined meaning for astrologers – of drawing up an annual revolution of a nativity. Furthermore, such an activity demonstrates how astrology united personal identity and environmental factors, and how astrologers could make assessments about one's future based upon interpretation of one's time of birth. Destiny was encoded within identity across time.

These annual revolutions were not merely performed for individuals. This annual speculative figure was also set for the world itself, and so called a *Figura Mundi*. Geneva provides an excellent description of this activity:

> 'political astrologers computed the celestial situation at the time of the world's yearly 'birthday', the first day of spring, when the sun entered Aries. This world figure... was used by astrologers to make predictions for the fate of the entire society, its rulers and ruling classes, harvest, plagues, famine, weather, as well as for 'the people' – anything likely to affect the society as a whole.'[200]

It was this figure that almanac-writing astrologers made most use of to draw up their national and international

---

200 Geneva, p. 179.

appraisals and prognostications. Lilly based his *Merlinus Anglicus Junior* of 1644 on such a figure of the heavens at the time of this 'Ingresse of the Sun into the first point of *Aries*'.[201] In this figure Mercury (described as 'the father of lyes and untruths') is to be found in Pisces ('a Common signe') which tells us that it will 'all this whole yeare... vex us with flying reports, continuall feares, false alarums, untoward speeches, contradictory news, lying messengers, and cozening Accomptants, Receivers, Treasurers, and the like'.[202] The overt but non-specific political implications of this statement highlight the status of astrologers as political surveyors. They announced the total character of the year's political affairs. Crucially, interpretation of the *figura mundi* demonstrates again how astrology created meaning by exploring natural interrelations of human political phenomena and the environment.

The other crucial astrological activity to have a bearing on the political contexts of early modern life was the expressly political applications of horary questions and their resolutions. Ashmole made notes of figures he cast which often related to political concerns – a figure cast on the 20th January 1648 asks 'whether the King shall be restored and whether his life be not in danger'.[203] Ashmole also kept a close watch on the movements of the planets to deduce general political mood and direction – between 7th and 31st January 1674 he 'wrote notes on events in Parliament... accompanied by references to current astrological constellations'.[204] Moreover, Ashmole

---

201   Lilly, *Merlinus Anglicus Junior* (London, 1644), p. 2-3.

202   Ibid, p. 4.

203   MS Ashm. 1136, f. 184v; cited in Josten, p. 467.

204   Josten, p. 1362; citing MS. Ashm. 436, ff. 24v, 24.

seems even to have been asked for astrological council by Charles II himself, who had 'asked Ashmole to calculate and to interpret a horoscope for the time at which he began his speech at the opening of Parliament on 27 October 1673.'[205] Likewise, many leaders and prominent figures of radical sects, not to mention Parliamentarians, consulted astrologers about how their particular political struggles would fare, and there was 'well-documented recourse to astrologers by radicals of all kind'.[206] It hardly seems surprising, given the ease with which astrology could literally pluck political assessment out of the sky. Astrological questioning into political matters was a means of generating information; themes, symbols and relations to be interpreted and applied to the situation at hand. Furthermore, this ritual of questioning and answering was initiated by referring to a chart created at the very point of astrological intervention – when the astrologer was posed the question. This practice was explained on the grounds that 'as the *Nativity* is the time of the Birth of the Body, *the Horary Question* is the time of the Birth of the Minde'.[207] The querent themselves was responsible for the timing of questioning, which (through horary ritual) would produce a snapshot of the astrological forces currently at work. The astrological action revealed knowledge and an understanding of the situation in question that could facilitate further and better action.

---

205 Josten, p. 1351, n 1; citing a letter from Lilly to Ashmole (MS. Rawl. D. 864, ff. 61-62v) and the figure that Ashmole cast for the speech which included comparisons to the king's nativity (MS. Ashm. 436, f. 10v).

206 Thomas, p. 443. For more on astrological consultation by various radicals see Thomas, p. 443-9.

207 John Gadbury, *The Doctrine of Nativities* (London, 1658), ii, p. 235.

Political speculation in astrology was not always
explicitly voiced. Criticisms of the incumbent regime
couched in the symbolic language of astrology could slip
past the censors but be understood by readers aware of
astrological symbolism and cipher conventions. Lilly
adopted a technique of substituting the name or direct
mention of King Charles with the 10th house of the
heavens, the *Medium Coeli*.[208] Likewise, in his *Anglicus*
for 1645, Lilly explained the ascendant (the first house of
the heavens) represented the people as a whole. He even
went on to explain that such significations could be used
to astrologically determine, during 'turbulent times, if...
the successe [would belong] to King or People.'[209] Geneva
cites Lilly's January 1644 interpretation of the *figura mundi*
and judges that Lilly was using this interpretation 'to cast
doubt in a covert manner on the public benefit of the peace
articles' negotiated secretly between King and Parliament,
which became public knowledge by December 1643.[210]
Lilly's interpretation (in the final printed version) claims
that the peace articles, represented astrologically by Venus
and Jupiter, 'behold the tenth house with trine aspect,
which is of love and affection: but I say... neither Venus or
Jupiter do behold the ascendant... the Articles themselves
shall have more in them, which may advance the desires of
those signified by Medium Coeli, th[a]n the good of the
people signified by the ascend[ant]'.[211] Lilly was making a
political astrological analysis of the treaty as favouring the

---

208   He explained in his *Merlinus Anglicus Junior*, 'when i speake of the
      tenth house, I intend somewhat of Kings'. William Lilly, *Anglicus
      Junior*; cited in Geneva p. 181

209   William Lilly, *Anglicus* (London, 1645); cited in Geneva p. 181.

210   Geneva, p. 184.

211   Lilly, *Anglicus* (1644), p. 5-6; cited in Geneva, p. 186.

King more than "the People". Such an opinion is confirmed by Geneva's citation of earlier manuscript versions of this interpretation, where Lilly unveils his coded language: 'the tenth house representing his Maty: and the ascendant the Parl'.[212] Specific references to the King and Parliament were excised from the final print version, allowing the document to slide under the radar of Presbyterian censors while still being understood by those aware of the cipher key.

This substitution ciphering was not limited to a few astrologically savvy practitioners – such substitutions would have been well understood by many people.[213] Even if the codes were occluded enough to pass by censors, 'judging... from the sales figures the public were not so slow-witted.'[214] Substitution not only refined the accuracy of interpretation, but meant that astrology could operate as a secret code language. Coding creates cases where action requires knowledge. One must know the code to be able to unlock it – and to use it for one's own purposes. Through coding, astrology made itself politically necessary. It could be criticised, but if it was used by one's enemies it must nevertheless be used to decipher their information. On the battlefields of civil war cryptography and intelligence, where astrology was a weapon employed by both sides, knowledge and action were intrinsically linked.[215]

212　Cited in Geneva, p. 185.

213　For example, George Thomason annotates the chart explaining significations of the houses in his edition of Lilly's 1644 *Anglicus* with 'Charles' in the tenth house and 'Parlemt' in the first house, the ascendant, which Geneva calls a 'smoking gun for this sort of study'. Geneva, p. 181.

214　Geneva, p. 186. For more sales figures, see Capp, *Astrology,* p. 44.

215　See also the section on propaganda, Chapter 3.

INTERPRETATION

In their role as interpreters of the heavens, astrologers were in a unique position to offer interpretations of both the natural development of events and of divine favour or wrath. The main means of dissemination of judicial astrology was the almanac, which was 'after the Bible, by far the most popular kind of literature in seventeenth-century England.'[216] Along with guidelines and advice on weather and agriculture, almanacs contained specific predictions about the resolution of particular political events. After all, 'natural sympathy or concord (antonym = antipathy/ discord) between human microcosms and the universal macrocosm underscored a universal interdependence, rendering individual morality relevant to the state of the commonwealth, just as the position of the stars influenced events in the world and personal behavior.'[217] Astrology could not only give explanation for the underlying mechanics of politics, but actually offer moral judgements on both an eventual outcome and how best to respond.

In a 1660 speech to the houses of Parliament, the author – whom Rachum suggests was politician Edward Hyde (1609-1674), 'the man who had successfully negotiated Charles II's return')[218] – lays out a thoroughly astrological explanation of the Interregnum upheaval of the old royalist order and the Restoration return of monarchy. The speech initially lays out an exoneration of the republican behaviour of the nation as

---

216 Curry, p. 21. Indeed, John Gaule complained that English people preferred 'to look and commune of their almanacs, before the Bible.' Thomas, p. 353; citing J. Gaule, The *Mag-Astro-Mancer* (London, 1652), sig. A3.

217 David Lederer, *Madness, Religion and the State in Early Modern Europe* (Cambridge, 2006), p. 31.

218 Rachum, 'The Term 'Revolution'', p. 877.

a whole, insisting 'Let us not be too much ashamed... [for]
The *Astrologers* have given us a fair excuse, and truly I hope
a true one; all the motions of these last Twenty years have
been unnatural, and have proceeded from the evil influence
of a malignant Star'.[219] Such a celestial harbinger of disorder
had affected 'the humor, and the temper, and the nature of
our Nation.' There was to be a minimum of recrimination,
partly because the deviant actions of the Republic were
beyond the responsibility of individuals, and partly because
this evil had now run its course – 'the same *Astrologers* assure
us, that the malignity of that Star is expired; the good *genius*
of this Kingdom is become Superior, and hath mastered that
malignity, and our own good old Stars govern us again'.[220]
Monarchism had 'mastered' republicanism, exactly as the
old stars had vanquished this recent astrological malignancy.

Sensibility and order had returned with the good old
stars, 'and their influence is so strong, that with our help,
they will repair in a year what hath been decaying in twenty'.
Now was to be a time of rebuilding, not of finger-pointing.
Such an astrological characterisation of events allowed an
absolution of the grievances of the civil war, yet it also
laid down a line in the sand on this amnesty. Those who
continued their radical disruptive activity and 'malignity',
who now 'have no excuse from the Star... [would] own all the
ill that is past to be their own, by continuing and improving
it for the time to come.'[221] The past twenty years could be
excused as a brief madness, in which the nation had taken
leave of its senses under the influence of evil stars, but those
who persisted in disruptive or treasonous activity would

219   *A collection of His Majesties gracious letters, speeches, messages and
      declarations since April 1660* (London, 1660), p. 70.

220   Ibid, p. 71.

221   Ibid, p. 70-71.

now have no such insanity plea to protect them. This was an astrological ultimatum issued by the resumed royalist order to the former dissenters – the time of civil unrest and panic was over, order had been restored, and anyone continuing this fit of temporary national insanity would be personally prolonging damaging behaviour and held fully accountable. Astrology provided political assessment both exoneration and subsequent potential culpability. Blaming past stars also abnegated guilt whilst stressing a renewed sense of responsibility.

It would be a severe disservice to astrology's contribution to language to say that it merely provided particular words or definitions. Astrology could identify forces that underpinned political events – indeed the same forces underlying the universal totality of events – and was therefore able to analyse particular expressions of those forces in a systemised methodology of observation and interpretation. Astrology could even locate, identify and justify particular significances of *and from* occurring events. Its universal scope allowed particular political events to be analysed for general assessment of political zeitgeist, as well as observations of general trends to be distilled into predictions of particular activity. Astrology actually framed discourses of political speculation, simultaneously interconnecting both the environment and the individual to form political assessment, speculation and judgement.

PROPAGANDA

Astrological characterisations of the meaning of events had powerful effects on seventeenth-century politics. The astrologer almanac-writers occupied a privileged position as potent political interpreters for the public. These interpretations were a key use of astrology – 'their effect on the national morale was great... the role of the astrologer as a propagandist during the decade of turbulence from 1640 to 1650 became both significant and profitable.'[222] Astrological readings and judgements of political events were certainly not an invention of the early modern period, yet meanings derived from particular conjunctions had been traditionally couched in generalisations. These generalisations of classical astrological meanings were made specific in this period of political instability and uncertainty: 'where the textbook states that a particular conjunction foreshadowed the death of a ruler, or some upheaval in the church, the almanac-maker was willing to publish a specific and partisan judgement on an individual, party or sect.'[223] Astrology offered particular and definitive political projections, speculations, and analyses that were used for expressly political ends.

Astrologers could offer assurances of victory through assessment of figures, as in the case of Lilly and Wharton's differing astrological interpretations of the king's march from Oxford.[224] This was far from an isolated incident. Lilly's almanac for 1646 contained the judgement that 'some shattered Brigade of his Majesties may move West or Norwest ; they have ill successe, as the [quartile] of [Saturn] and [Mars] tells me'.[225] Such a prediction had a double effect in strengthening the resolve of Parliament and their

---

222   Rusche, 'Astrology and Propaganda', p. 322.

223   Capp, *Astrology*, p. 58-9.

224   See section on interpretation, Chapter 3..

225   William Lilly, *Anglicus... for 1646*, (London, 1645/6), p. B2v-B3. Although Rusche also uses this passage in his article he makes a slight misquotation, calling the quartile a conjunction (Rusche, 'Astrology and Propaganda', p. 326). The significance of this error is apparent when we know that the quartile 'is of enmity and not good', whereas a conjunction 'is good or bad, according to the nature of the question demanded.' Lilly, *Christian Astrology*, p. 26-7.

supporters whilst simultaneously weakening that of the Royalists.[226] Assurances for one side were, of course, also warnings to the other.

Another type of astrological political speculation was the study of ruler's nativities. This was somewhat of a risky business – laws prohibited the calculation or consideration of such genitures, and several practitioners were imprisoned for just this.[227] The illegality of such activity itself provides us with an idea of how powerful such a practice was considered. Calculating a regent's life expectancy was 'in popular estimation... not far removed from malevolent conjuration to take away the ruler's life.'[228] Gadbury admits that 'The Politician takes cognizance of the great dangers, and eminent disadvantages[,] the making known a Princes destiny may do him.'[229] Astrology was dangerous not because it was inherently diabolic or evil but because it was a powerful tool. Here was an early modern grasp of an interrelation of knowledge and action, and of foreknowledge and effect, as well as of astrology and magic. The nativity figure *did* hold enciphered symbols that could be related to the native's time and manner of death: Lilly describes the eighth House's 'nature and signification' as 'Death, its quality and nature... What kinde of Death a Man shall dye'.[230] Perhaps because of this concern, it was considered more acceptable to publish an exact geniture once the native was deceased, which supported

226   Rusche, 'Astrology and Propaganda', p. 326.

227   Curry, p. 47.

228   Thomas, p. 407.

229   John Gadbury, *The Nativity of the late King Charls* (London, 1659), sig. A4v.

230   Lilly, *Christian Astrology*, p. 54.

an astrological practice of analysing recent political history
using the nativity figures of recent rulers. Gadbury's
Nativity of the late King Charls was subtitled *with Reasons in
Art Of the Various Success, and Mis-fortune of His Whole Life* –
tellingly, it was further subtitled 'a brief History of our late
unhappy Wars.' Astrology once more united the individual
and the events surrounding them. It described history
as the actions of people, and analysed them by mapping
influences of divine forces.

Astrological interpretation was used to spin nativities
to fit particular assessments of the ruler's character.
Royalist Gadbury's 'general judgment' for Charles' nativity
considers the chart to 'Astrologically demonstrate the
temperature of this native to be Sanguine Cholerique;
which humors prevailing, argued him to be of disposition
and behavior courteous, and affable, yet Princelike,
magnanimous and imperious.'[231] In contrasting opinion but
with similar technique, Lilly judged of the king, 'He had
the signe *Leo* ascending in his Nativity... which made him
so obstinate.'[232] Re-prioritisation of emphasis in nativity
analysis could yield wildly different characterisations of
rulers. Astrological knowledge could provide "proofs"
for opposing interpretations, each of which would have a
political effect and reaction. Explanation of the strengths
or weaknesses of a ruler was a political action facilitated by
astrological knowledge.

The personality of the monarch was explained by the
nativity figure for expressly political reasons. Reasonably
enough, the personalities of rulers (particularly the
powerful ones of pre-modern times) are still held to be
an important part of political analysis. Thomas makes

---

231   Gadbury, *The Nativity of the late King*, p. 14.

232   Lilly, *Monarchy or No Monarchy*, p. 56.

comment on both the function and importance of this
political psychology of astrology:

'In an age of near-absolute monarchy the attention
paid to the horoscopes of royal princes was fully
justified. The political history of a nation could to
some extent be explained in terms of the individual
psychology of its rulers.'[233]

These astrological assessments of the personalities,
proclivities, foibles and idiosyncrasies of political leaders
were not simply *ad hominem* attacks, although certainly this
was also popular. When speaking of powerful autocrats, the
personal(ity) was the political.

The sheer utility and power of astrology meant that
'during the civil war Royalists and Parliamentarians alike
exploited the propaganda value of astrological predictions'.[234]
In order to repudiate negative judgements it became
necessary to use an astrologer to catch an astrologer. Rusche
conjures a wonderful image of an occult dimension to the
civil war: 'while the armies of King Charles and parliament
fought in the fields, the astrologers chose to defend their
causes with their almanacs in the personal and vitriolic battle
of words.'[235] This battle of words between astrologers was
not restricted to interpretation, but also to critical analysis
of the work of other astrologers. Wharton criticised Lilly
and fellow Roundhead astrologer, John Booker, saying 'art
not you [Booker] and Mr. *Lilly* alike ashamed, to account
your selves Masters in *Astrology*, when... neither of you have

---

233   Thomas, p. 385.

234   Capp, *Astrology*, pp. 21, 72-88.

235   Rusche, 'Astrology and propaganda', p. 322.

yet attained so much skill, as to set a Figure of Heaven exactly?'[236] Much of this conflict was made up of slander and personal attacks: for example, the satirical altering of Wharton's anagrammatic pen-name "Naworth" to "No-worth".[237] Such attacks were more than childish squabbling. Upon the battlegrounds of rival almanacs, the political had become the personal, for 'to attack the man was to attack his ability to defend his political position.'[238]

Astrological propaganda highlights the importance of the astrologer's role as interpreter of the divine ordering. Their interpretations were, politically, very useful. Astrologers offered assurances of victory, justifications of political acts, political assessments of recent events, and counter-analysis and refutations against the astrological propaganda efforts of one's enemies. This activity was backed up by interpretations of divine favour for whichever side that particular astrologer backed. Lilly is unselfconscious in announcing in the postscript to *The Starry Messenger*: 'God is on our side ; the Constellations of Heaven after a while will totally appeare for the Parliament'.[239] Astrological knowledge of divine underlying forces informed and justified political action. It thereby linked not only politics and religion, but also humanity with its environment – our political ordering and activity was a rung on a ladder bridging the individual and the entire universe happening with (rather than merely around) us.

---

236 John Gadbury (ed.), *The Works of George Wharton* (London, 1683), p. 239.

237 For more on this biting character assassination see ibid, p. 275.

238 Rusche, 'Astrology and propaganda', p. 323.

239 Lilly, *The Starry Messenger*, postscript.

POLITICAL CONCLUSIONS

What is evident from this study is that astrologers were more than assessors – they were interpreters. They were analysts, deriving detail from stylised data-sets, and their focus was the future. They were to be experts on foreknowledge of all kinds. Astrology was itself after all a form of prophecy. Their skills of interpretation and reinterpretation allowed generalised knowledge to be specified into a forecast of a specific outcome. This was especially useful in political judicial work. Prophecy, and astrology in general, characterised politics in a language of symbols and analogy. Different astrological interpretations of events were methods of modelling not only the political subject (be it event, group, individual or mood) but the universal totality of contexts in which the subject existed. Religious as well as occult knowledge informed political action via astrological knowledge. Political contexts were dependent upon a co-mingled religious, environmental and magical discourse. Astrologers were intermediaries between divine underlying cosmic processes and the organisation of human affairs.

Astrological knowledge was not interested in scientifically provable abstract truth value – or rather, it already assumed the hidden but theologically imminent truth value of astrological correspondences. It was interested in how this astrological knowledge was utilised, what function it performed, how it contributed to or detracted from what it analysed, explained and interpreted. When astrology explained historical processes and recent events, it was affecting the subject of its study through its positive and negative assessments. Natural portents characterised political organisations and therefore fostered judgements of and reactions to them, while astrological propaganda had an

affect on what it measured or talked about – intentionally
aiding the culmination and fruition of their predictions.
Astrological modelling shaped perception, understanding
and, ultimately, further action. The extent of this can be
seen in the ways in which astrology made itself politically
necessary through substitution codes and counter-astrology.
The action of deciphering and answering the interpretations
of one's rivals depended upon astrological knowledge.

Astrology analysed the shifting foundations of politics,
offering insider information on the way political events
were developing. It interpreted the continuum of political
contexts as a multitudinous series of cycles, constantly
beginning and ending. Beginning gave a new opportunity
to examine the astrological factors surrounding political
events through horary consultation and election. Endings
of old influences stressed a new sense of responsibility,
and themselves gave way to new beginnings, for astrology
had no place for vacuums. Political horary astrology used
knowledge to affect situations through interpreting and
analysing. The political activities of astrologers during the
civil war highlight how tangible action was just as much a
part of being an astrologer as predicting and printing.

So astrology combined the specific practicalities of
analysis and action with the abstract universalities of religious
and spiritual occult principles concerning the nature of
God, the ordering of His creation, and (most importantly)
how all these things would fit together in the future. As
intermediaries, the religious role of astrologers could stray
dangerously close to that of priests, even interpreting and
espousing their own Scriptural truths. We see this especially
in the various exegeses of Revelations by pamphleteers and
almanac-writers.[240] Prophecy and astrology were a potent

---

240 For example, John Booker, *The Bloody Almanack.*

combination – prophecy benefitted from astrology's ability to provide justifications and specificity using a wealth of symbolic taxonomies, and astrology benefitted from the prestige and popularity of prophecy.

Even beyond theological exegesis, the delineations between the roles of priest and magician in a naturally magical world frequently overlapped. The clergyman, astrologer and magician Richard Napier did not simply carry out these roles as separate and discrete interests; they were frequently combined and interrelated to inform and strengthen the functions he was called upon to perform.[241] As we shall see later, there are cases of seventeenth-century priests actually carrying out their astrological calculations upon their church altars, combining their occult and spiritual activities in the same consecrated physical spaces, utilising the same sacred equipment.[242] The astrologer relied on models and principles of God's plan that were magical *and* religious. This is not to suggest astrology attempted to usurp established Christian religion, rather that it existed as a parallel to the Church as a practical Christian spiritual practice. Astrology worked towards discovering and interpreting the divine imperative in specific human action, and particular political organisations of human life.

The civil wars offer a variety of cases of the desirability of such discovery and interpretation. There are frequent requests from both sides of the conflicts for astrologers to give straightforward prognostications about whether particular political endeavours would be successful, such as Charles II's consultation with Ashmole. There were also calls for clarifications and verifications. In a section of Lilly's astrological handbook, *Christian Astrology*, entitled

---

241   See section on mind, body, and soul, Chapter 4.

242   See section on personal consultancy, Chapter 4.

'If a Report or common Rumour were True or False', Lilly presents, as a working example of such a verification method, a figure of the heavens at 4:31 p.m. on 11th April 1643 analysed to ascertain whether accounts 'that his Majesty had taken Cambridge': from the evidence of, *inter alia*, the square aspect of Saturn and Mars, he judged the rumours false.[243] Astrologers were not simply long-sighted soothsayers proclaiming vague final outcomes: they were up-to-date providers of information on shifting battlefields where accurate reconnaissance was scarce and quick decisions required.

To consider both the magic and rationality of such consultations, we can study in more detail the case of Lilly's work for prominent Leveller leader Richard Overton, answering 'whether, by joining with the agents of the private soldiery of the Army for the redemption of common right and freedom to the land and removal of oppressions from the people, my endeavours shall be prosperous or no'.[244] Thomas points out that Overton was hardly thought a "superstitious" man: indeed, he quotes P. Zagorin's assessment that the radical leader was a firm 'rationalist' who rejected dogmatic unquestioning belief.[245] Overton's note of April 1648 asking for Lilly's expert astrological opinion cannot therefore be regarded simply as the actions of a simple, gullible or "backwards" man, but rather a rational decision-maker taking full advantage of every means at his disposal to investigate and analyse a complex and shifting political situation.[246]

---

243 Lilly, *Christian Astrology*, p. 199-201

244 Ashm. 420, attached to f. 267

245 Thomas, p. 372

246 Thomas considers that 'there is no stronger testimony to the appeal

The recourse to astrological investigation and analysis itself was also an act requiring certain inherently magical ideas about the generation of knowledge through understanding occult virtues in time, and even of underlying interrogations of fate and destiny. The ritual of horary astrology invested the querent themselves directly in the process of divination – the time they put their question to the astrologer was the "random input" element necessary for divinatory knowledge-generation. This very process highlighted deeply occult principles underlying astrological practice: everything was connected, reflected and reflecting. There was in fact no "randomness" when it came to destiny, merely the time ordained to act – to enquire and to decide – encoded within which was an understanding waiting to be unfolded. Determining a correct time, as in election, and deciphering such a time's meaning, as in horary work, were intensely political acts.

Astrology's magical roots also nourished the political usage of images, amulets and other enchantment – perhaps the most obviously magical of the occult means by which one could harness astrological forces to one's benefit. Just like the astrological images used in agriculture, images could also be constructed at appropriate times to bring to the bearer various political advantages. They could be made for the benefit of a particular government so as to 'causeth nobleness, height of a kingdom, and greatness of dominion'[247] or to 'giveth

---

of astrological advice in the mid seventeenth century than this request'. Thomas, p. 372

247   'in the second face [of Aries] ascendeth a form of a woman, outwardly clothed with a red garment, and under it a white, spreading abroad over her feet, and this image causeth nobleness, height of a kingdom, and greatness of dominion' Agrippa, *Three Books*, p. 377

power, nobility, and dominion over people'[248] to ambitious individuals. These astrological images could also be used to bring occult aid to the disenfranchised and oppressed, as with the image of the first face [decan] of Libra:

'...the form of an angry man, in whose hand is a pipe, and the form of a man reading in a book; the operation of this is in justifying and helping the miserable and weak against the strong and powerful and wicked...'[249]

Such political utilities of talismanic objects also included forms of magical sabotage: an amulet of the twenty-fourth mansion of the Moon could be used 'for the victory of soldiers', yet it also 'hurteth the execution of government'.[250]

Politics existed within a magical framework of reality, and was subject to the liminal forces that governed the individual as an expression of nature. Magic was the hidden physics of divine nature, and astrology merely another means to categorise and therefore comprehend and manipulate it. Politics is sometimes defined as processes for determining the best acquisition and use of resources. By this kind of understanding, the early modern magical universe was certainly politicised in a number of magical

---

248 '...in the second face [of Taurus] ascendeth a naked man, holding in his hand a key; it giveth power, nobility, and dominion over people' Agrippa, *Three Books*, p. 377

249 Agrippa, *Three Books*, p. 378

250 'The twenty-fourth [Mansion of the Moon] is called Sadabath or Chadezoad, that is the Star of Fortune; it is prevalent for the benevolence of married folk, for the victory of soldiers, it hurteth the execution of government, and hindereth that it may not be exercised.' Agrippa, *Three Books*, p. 369

ways. The Great Chain of Being essentialised a naturally hierarchical understanding of power, and by extension the mandate to wield it, as emanating and descending from God the Highest through to humans. Whether one distinguished different rungs on the ladder for different humans made the difference between divine right and mortal equanimity before the Almighty.[251]

Astrology mapped essential natures in an interrelated context of influences. The nature of literally any phenomenon existed in relation to the surrounding forces which could be mapped by the movement and influence of the stars. Celestially-influenced predispositions of individuals and groups to certain behaviour or outcomes could be used to inform the astrologer about distinct culminations of these moods into particular events. Likewise, these particular events could be analysed to extrapolate an assessment of a larger astrological picture. Early modern English politics owed a lot to this astrological picture, for it was a picture of the universe and how humans regulate, have regulated and would continue to regulate themselves and their affairs.

Political astrology took example from the rule of nature by the stars. Curry divides astrology of this period into elite types, characterised by Ashmole and the autocratic and authoritarian doctrine of inferiors being forced to obey

---

251 For more on such religious equanimity see, for one set of examples, the various works on the seventeenth-century radicals known as the Ranters: A.L. Morton, *The World of the Ranters* (London, 1970); Christopher Hill, *The Word Turned Upside Down* (London, 1972; 1991 reprint) especially chapters 8, 9, 10 and 15; Jerome Friedman, *Blasphemy, Immorality, and Anarchy* (Ohio, 1987); E.P. Thompson, 'On the Rant' in Eley and Hunt (ed.), *Reviving the English Revolution* (London, 1988); Byron Nelson, 'The Ranters and the Limits of Language', in Holstun (ed.) *Pamphlet Wars: Prose in the English Revolution* (London, 1992); Ariel Hessayon, *'Gold tried in the Fire': The Prophet TheaurauJohn Tany and the English Revolution* (Ashgate, 2007).

superiors, and democratic types, characterised by Lilly and his maxim *'non cogunt'* – that the stars incline, but do not compel.[252] Whether an invisible iron fist or a gentle helping hand, seventeenth-century politics recognised the touch of the stars in all of life, especially national political life. Astrology understood politics by looking at how individual and environment interrelated in a mutually cohesive and symbolically demonstrable relationship. Astrologers interpreted symbols to form a comprehensive discourse, which worded discussion, analysis and judgement of political contexts in the language of social and environmental contexts.

Natural portents were assessed against an individual's nativity chart to locate significant correlations, contrasts and emphases. Similarly, the freeze-framed star-map of a nativity was manipulated to reveal secrets about the native's relations with the world – the figure revolved forward to portray actions in the coming year. Astrological enquiry sought after an idea of destiny encoded within individual identity – the nativity was an outline of birth's threshold between the personal and the environmental. Politics was both a process of individuals being swept along by vast underlying forces, and also the manifestation of human avatars of these divine forces. A political actor could come to represent the astrological forces that characterised them, as a crystallisation of these influences in physical interaction with the universe and humanity's ordering of it. This was an astrological explanation of politics as the striving of groups as well as individuals to affect their environment. Astrology also looked to the environment for its influence upon political affairs. Analysis of the *figura mundi* extrapolated and interpreted political significance from the turning of the year. The environment was studied

252   Curry, chapter 2.

to provide insight into the nature of all things – especially politics. This was the complementary astrological view of politics as the dynamics of nature affecting groups and therefore individuals. In this early modern astrology everything affects everything else all the time.

Overall, politics was an expression of complexity in this universal astrological system of meaning. Politically-minded astrology was a total investigative system that mapped the actions of individuals and groups. What politics searches for, especially upon the verge and in the midst of great actions that will affect many – such as civil war, the Commonwealth, and even Restoration of the old regime – is explanation, analysis, assessment and, above all, justification. Astrologers provided a vital service in the political contexts of seventeenth-century England, precisely by using a system that united all contexts.

CHAPTER 4
THE SOCIAL

ASTROLOGICAL KNOWLEDGE AND ACTION AFFECTED conceptions of different scales of meaning – the nature of time, eschatology and destiny – and ideas about how a magical universe affected human life. Finally therefore, we come to the social contexts within which astrology operated. These social contexts consist of two areas. There is what we can call societal astrology – the exploration of astrological forces and influences underlying human society as a whole. This included judicial astrology that looked to the forces underpinning politics itself and explored astrological considerations of society as a more foundational level of complexity. It made pronouncements about the essence of society, how social developments would unfold, and by what fundamental principles it operated.

The second area could be called personal astrology, and concerned itself with resolving individuals' personal issues. This type of social astrology included the services, assistance and advice astrological practitioners offered to clients. Personal astrology ranged from divination to finding lost or stolen property to counsel over all kinds of personal problems. Crucially, it also offered various solutions to the problems it could detect and explain. This function of astrology was the key to the most popular and important form of personal astrology – medical diagnosis, prognosis and treatment.

Astrology explored the universal undercurrents of human existence and experience. Social astrology covers both the outlining of temperaments of an individual, and

developments of society as a whole, because it conceived
the two as united. It analysed individuals as forming
complexes of social interrelations, and considered these
individuals within a total context – providing theories
and techniques important for analysing everyday personal
life and for mass social trends and events. As the stars
predispose or "tempt" individuals, so the society those
individuals make up experiences particular social, political
and economic phenomena.

The manner in which individual and society reflect
each other is also profoundly magical. The microcosmic
activity and passivity of the human scale was used to model
the macrocosmic processes and behaviours of society – just
as the practice of the revolution of a person's nativity chart
was also utilised in the *figura mundi* to tell of the world's
fate. This anthropocentric evidence base for understanding
the cosmos was based on the occult principles emphasising
the fundamental natural unity of all scales, human and
universal. The actions of the stars would excite particular
behaviours from a kingdom just as they would an individual.
This influence on and of individuals is at the root of all
social astrology.

We observe in social astrology the unification and
intermingling of the three strands of this book's assessment.
The ways in which knowledge affects action, the cross-
pollination and fusing of astrology and magic, and the ways
astrology linked individual and environment in a grand scope
of human meaning all begin to merge at this most personal
of levels. This environmental influence on the personal and
interpersonal contexts includes both the environment of
one's immediate surroundings and of the entire cosmos.

SOCIETAL ASTROLOGY

As we have seen, the early modern definition of the natural world included the actions and impact of human phenomena of all kinds. Events that our modern assessment might deem socio-economic, as well as 'sweeping political and religious changes'[253], were considered to be kinds of natural disasters which could be predicted by astrological activity. However, societal astrology did not solely concern itself with these sudden sweeping changes. It was also interested in developing relatively subtle speculation on social theory. While headmaster and early meteorologist John Goad (1616-1689) is often mentioned, like Jeake, for keeping records of weather conditions, it has also been remarked that he 'must have been one of the earliest writers to notice that suicide rates vary according to the time of the year.'[254] Goad reasoned that such a phenomenon could be explained astrologically, given that the planets affected the weather and 'as the Physician knows the *Delirium* of his Feavourish Patient is heightened by the Intemperance of the Weather.'[255] Societal astrology dealt with a social phenomenon such as suicide by examining astrological influences upon the individual, then following this influence up into general social theory.

Goad had 'observed various *Alterations* and *Emotions* of Spirit under [conjunctions of] [Saturn] [Jupiter], Visible in *Melancholly, Griefs, Distractions, Phrensies, Lunacies, &c.*'[256] He conjectured that 'those unhappy *Felo's de-se*, that make

---

253   Curry, p. 8.

254   Thomas, p. 388; citing John Goad, *Astrometeorologica* (London, 1686), p. 506-7. For more on treatment for suicidal patients, see section on mind, body, and soul, Chapter 4.

255   Goad, p. 506.

256   Ibid.

away themselves by what kind so ever; I do suspect are the worse... through the Potency of the [Saturn-Jupiter] configuration'.[257] Many psychological afflictions were held to be capable of causing bodily malfunction in early modern England, and could even be fatal. It was not uncommon during this period to list a cause of death as 'grief', 'despair', 'fright', or even a broken heart.[258] John Graunt's study of the Bills of Mortality claims that in 1632, 11 die of 'Grief', 5 of 'Lunatique' and, particularly pertinent to our study, 13 are simply listed as being killed by 'Planet'.[259] The influence of the planets was thought powerful enough to be able to predispose to fatality on occasion.

Goad put forward the idea that, far from separate phenomena, fatal psychological conditions (such as early modern conceptions of grief) might be considered different expressions of an overall form of unbalanced mental health, a conclusion reached in part by noticing that 'Grief, Lunacy, and the Melancholly *Desperado* are carried forth in the same Weekly Sheet to be buryed.'[260] Time as viewed using astrological symbolism and enciphering could itself be utilised as a critical tool for assessing human lives, particularly the circumstances and factors influencing the actions of people who deliberately ended theirs. Goad declared a link between a particular sort of personal human event and the

---

257   Ibid. He also noted that 'I cannot deny... that other Aspects may sometimes be unhappy, but I chance to observe it first in [Saturn] [Jupiter]'. Goad, p. 507.

258   MacDonald, *Mystical Bedlam*, p. 182.

259   John Graunt, *Natural and Political Observations mentioned in a following Index, and made upon the Bills of Mortality* (London, 1662), p. 9. 'To be thus "planet-struck" or "blasted" was to be suddenly and inexplicably affected by a paralyzing disease, apoplexy, or other kind of sudden death.' Thomas, p. 75.

260   Goad, p. 507.

astrological influence that underlay the passage of time. He collected and presented cases of periods of high suicide rates, and also observed periods of non-activity.[261] He was quick to point out he was not positing a simple causal relationship between suicide and particular planetary aspects.[262] Rather, that 'Minds, Sickly, and Crazy, and Distemper'd by our natural Weakness... are not able to stand under the harsher temptations of the Planets.'[263] The stars inclined the natural tendencies of individuals (and humanity as a whole), but did not directly force the behaviours they prompted or encouraged. The use of the term "temptations" seems a particularly good indication of this assessment of the stars' exact influence. Nature obviously affected an individual – just as being wet and cold would encourage pneumonia, so exposure to the stars would doubtlessly affect a person's mood and mental state. Environment had a tangible effect on mental and physical balance. As we shall see later, early modern notions of mind and body (and therefore treatment of maladies) were complex and interrelated.[264] Likewise, we shall return to seventeenth-century suicide in the context of magical medicines, regimes and talismans.[265]

In early modern analysis of suicide, a topic which itself seemed to become less taboo across the period,[266] we can observe the universality of astrology's use as a tool

---

261 Ibid.

262 Goad, p. 506.

263 Ibid.

264 See section on mind, body, and soul, Chapter 4.

265 See the case of Gilbert Wright, in section on mind, body, and soul, Chapter 4.

266 For more on early modern suicide, see Michael MacDonald and T.R. Murphy, *Sleepless Souls* (Oxford, 1990), especially chapters 2-4, and p. 144-45.

for discussion and explanation. Goad was firm in his faith that 'even the Melancholly Secrets of Nature may be pryed into'.[267] From reproduction, to survival, to death, there was no aspect of human social existence that could not be interpreted using astrological techniques and symbolism. The comprehension of contexts of influence added to a growing compassionate appraisal of suicide. Furthermore the influences on social and psychological existence that astrological analysis could describe, model and predict were actually posited to underpin political events. As Goad asks in the rhetoric of an early modern astrologer and psychologist, 'what should I meddle with Discords, Tumults, Seditions, Wars, Rebellions, Treasons, Imposters, Sectaries, False-Prophets... all these proceed from a Diseased Mind and ungovern'd Passion, a Zeal that cannot be justified, Pride, Envy, Wrath, Heady, Hair-brain'd Temper, which... helps make Dangerous times'.[268] Politics was an expression of deeper factors shaping human existence; matters of material, social and psychological significance. Far from the stars "causing" a king to be killed, they represented the social forces that would lead to regicide. Thomas has stated that 'in their confident assumption that the principles underlying the development of human society were capable of human explanation, we can detect the germ of modern sociology'.[269] I would go further and suggest that astrology fulfilled the role and functions for early modern people that sociology and many other social sciences fulfil for us today. Instead of being considered proto-sociology, I would argue this kind of analysis and activity forms a fully fledged early

---

267   Goad, p. 506.

268   Goad, p. 507.

269   Thomas, p. 387.

modern sociology, one based upon astrological assumptions, tools and techniques rather than modern scientific ones. Astrology presented a system to understand and analyse all other systems. It was an interpretive craft that explained human existence and experience, and was dependent upon magical premises to explore, understand and manage the links between the individual and environment.

There is in Goad's analysis of suicide a certain admixture of what would previously have been called natural and judicial kinds of astrology. By instead examining astrology in particular contexts, in this case the social, we see that such distinctions are not easy to maintain. By attempting to understand and explain human endeavours and catastrophes of both personal and national scales, natural astrology informed conceptions of the very origins of the political contexts with which predictive judicial astrological activity concerned itself. To distinguish between natural and judicial one could say that natural astrology made predictions about general trends ("suicide rates will increase as Saturn enters conjunction with Jupiter") while judicial astrology made predictions about general events ("Scorpio's strong position shows the king will lose the war with Parliament"). The latter could be considered expressly socio-political, whereas the former was, in the broadest sense of the word, environmental. The term socio-political is a highly appropriate one, given the characteristic manner with which astrology assessed the politics of a particular time and the general laws and forces shaping society within the same analysis. The term "environmental" is used to indicate both the natural workings of nature, yet also to show that deeper environmental forces had a massive influence on how political events themselves were judged to be formulated from human social interaction. Any delineation between different forms of astrological methodology, such as attempting to distinguish between magical and empirical activities, must be aware of overlapping grounds. The search to understand natural processes was accompanied by a search for a beneficial outcome for human endeavour. Although theory and approach of natural and judicial might be separated by respective emphases upon empiricism and magic, they exist as bandwidths on a single astrological spectrum. Moreover, there is certainly crossover between the more "proto-scientific" natural astrology and more "magical" astrology in their practices, particularly when it came to actually doing something to alleviate the suffering of individuals.

HEALTH

Astrology was of central importance in early modern medicine. It was used as a diagnostic tool by clergymen, licensed physicians and the myriad "irregulars" who also practiced physic.[270] Astrological medicine concerned itself with understanding the nature of illness by studying how particular influences of the stars affected the patient. The most common astrological diagnostic techniques were either horary figures based on the time of consultation between patient and practitioner, or a decumbiture.[271] Whichever

---

270 Thomas, pp. 318, 354-5, 367-71; MacDonald, *Mystical Bedlam*, p. 8, 25, 175; Owen Davies, *Popular Magic: Cunning-Folk in English History* (London, 2007), p. 79-81. See also Allan Chapman, 'Astrological Medicine' in Webster (ed.), *Health, Medicine and Mortality in the Sixteenth Century* (Cambridge, 1979); Carroll Camden Jr., 'Elizabethan Astrological Medicine', in *Annals of Medical History*, 2 (1930), p. 217-26; Hugh G. Dick, 'Students of Physic and Astrology', *Journal of the History of Medicine*, 1-2 (1946), p. 300-315, 419-33; E.H. Hare, 'Medical Astrology and its Relation to Modern Psychiatry', *Proceedings of the Royal Society of Medicine*, 70 (February 1977), p. 105-10.

271 A map of the heavens for the time the patient had become ill.

technique was utilised, an up-to-date astrological map was essential, as the occult influences that astrological medicine analysed were considered to be in constant flux.[272] Astrologer-physicians such as Forman and Napier opted for casting by the time of consultation.[273] It was easier for the practitioner to note the time of consultation themselves because, as one contemporary noted, when it came it to the exact 'time of decumbiture... few know that'.[274] Astrological knowledge produced diagnoses from measurements determined by the time of astrological intervention. The horary 'ritual of interrogation'[275] was a prime example of divinatory analysis, which took data (stars' positions at the time of consultation or illness) and ran it through a systemised set of correspondences to discern information about the current composition of occult influences. Links between magic and astrology were also exemplified in the diagnostic use of geomancy, a divination system heavily based upon astrological symbolism.[276] Simon Forman is noted to have 'calculated an astrological, or on occasion a geomantical, figure for the time at which he was consulted and read this for the cause of the disease or to foresee its outcome.'[277]

---

272 Gowland, p. 23; Lederer, p. 33.

273 For Forman, see Lauren Kassell, 'Food of Angels', in *Secrets of Nature* (London, 2001), p. 372; for Napier, see MacDonald, *Mystical Bedlam*, p. 26.

274 George Atwell, *An Apology, Or, Defense of the divine art of Natural Astrology* (London, 1660), p. 26.

275 MacDonald, *Mystical Bedlam*, p. 26.

276 For more on the links between astrology and geomancy, see section on personal consultancy, Chapter 4.

277 Lauren Kassell, 'Food of Angels', p. 372. In reference to geomantic figures, Kassell elsewhere mentions that 'For Forman, alchemy and magic, along with astrology and geomancy, were kindred arts.' Kassell, 'Food of Angels', p. 367.

These medical charts of decipherable astrological symbolism were the early modern equivalents of blood tests and other modern diagnostic technologies.[278] Typically, a figure could be analysed in several ways: 'the sixth House, and his Lord [planet], signifies the sickness: the seventh the Physitian: the eighth Death : the tenth Medicine: the fourth the end of the Disease'.[279] A planet's position could be examined to yield information about the problem – '*Mars* in *Leo* afflicts the heart, the disease is a fever, and the cause of it choler.'[280] Lilly's *Christian Astrology* handbook also teaches how to analyse nativities for inherent susceptibility to certain conditions or illnesses.[281] This nativity analysis further highlights the ways astrology explored the links between one's situation and one's self.

Astrological figures provided essential information to be interpreted to pronounce both a diagnosis and prognosis of the sickness. Comparison with advanced modern medical technology is particularly appropriate when we understand that the main alternative diagnostic tool during the early modern period was uroscopy.[282] Astrology, in contrast, was a highly systemised practice with detailed operational parameters and a vast array of semiotic characterisations and models it could utilise. It simply provided more data that could be symbolically interpreted to produce useful information than the study of a patient's water. Napier

---

278   This analogy is also made in MacDonald, 'The Career of Astrological Medicine in England', p. 66.

279   Nicholas Culpeper, *Semeiotica Uranica* (London, 1658), p. 78.

280   Culpeper, *Semeiotica Uranica*, p. 104.

281   Lilly, *Christian Astrology*, pp. 129-30, 576-86.

282   i.e. examining a patient's urine to diagnose, pronounce prognosis and treat them. MacDonald, *Mystical Bedlam*, p. 29-30.

supported astrology over uroscopy on practical experiential grounds, claiming that, 'where his figure deceived him once, the urine did it ten times... And for that the Urine would not shew many things that the figure would'.[283]

When considering medical astrology we should also bear in mind the expectations of patients of the early modern period. It has been observed:

> 'seventeenth-century men and women were well aware of the feeble curative powers of contemporary medicine. What they expected above all from their doctors was that they distinguish fatal illnesses from harmless or transient maladies.'[284]

Forman's clients sometimes merely wanted him to pronounce whether their child would live or die, without apparently asking him to take any action to attempt to ensure the occurrence of the former rather than the latter: 'they simply wanted a prognosis.'[285] A figure of the heavens describing the underlying natural forces that had led to one's sickness would 'situate the patient in the cosmos, placing him at the vortex of the natural forces that impelled the universe, discovering the correspondences that linked microcosm and macrocosm.'[286] The medical astrologer was in a position to reconcile individual sickness, infirmity or bereavement with the larger cosmological picture, in a similar manner to the clergy. Yet they could also present the

---

283   Atwell, *An Apology*, p. 27.

284   MacDonald *Mystical Bedlam*, p. 29.

285   B.H. Traister, *The Notorious Astrological Physician of London: Works and Days of Simon Forman* (London, 2001), p. 64.

286   MacDonald, *Mystical Bedlam*, p. 26.

exact celestial mechanics that had created this sad state of affairs, and so held out a more comprehensible explanation than mere emphasis upon, say, God's mysterious nature. The role played by early modern astrological medical practitioners was as much that of a counsellor as it was a doctor of biology and medicine. The added importance of constructing a social meaning of disease and disorder should be appreciated in this light.

The medical figure of the heavens provided an initial case history for patients who suffered relapses. Forman encouraged other practitioners to 'look back to the first figure ever cast for the patient and to see if the signifiers (important astrological markers) of the cause of the disease had altered since the patient's first visit.'[287] The wealth of information that horary, nativity and decumbiture figures held was recorded for study of both current and similar future cases.[288] Beyond the immediate utility of a figure for diagnosis and treatment of the individual patient, such a record of the course of the infirmity added to the practitioner's stockpile of medical information to help better diagnose and treat future patients. Such records were in studious circulation between astrological medical practitioners. In a letter from astrologer-physician Arthur Dee (1579-1651) to Richard Napier, Dee discusses a collegial consultation he made with Napier concerning '*an fuisset gravida*' (whether a client was pregnant) and informs Napier 'we were both deceived, for it proved not so.' However, more than informing a consulting colleague of the conclusion of the case, Dee goes on to explain he has observed a particular trend that may be useful in future cases – Dee also included 'the figures to consider of it', and concluded his report by

---

287   Traister, p. 58.

288   MacDonald, *Mystical Bedlam*, p. 29.

asking Napier 'to send me some receipts of worth found by your own practice.'[289] We can observe here that the detailed analysis of such figures extended beyond diagnosis of an individual case into a wider inquiry into the refining and improvement of the practice of astrological medicine itself. Astrological knowledge about a particular incident was used to understand the whole system, and to better understand and manipulate future occurrences.

Once an astrological medical diagnosis had been made, a cure could be prescribed through planetary governorships: 'you may strengthen the part of the bodie by its like, as the brain by Herbs of *Mercury*' and, in addition, 'you may oppose diseases by Herbs of the Planet opposite to the Planet that causeth them, as... diseases of *Mars* by Herbs of *Venus*, and the contrarie'.[290] The 'occult vertues' afforded to natural resources by astrological governances could be applied to rebalance a patient's locus of astrological influences. By knowing the astrological signifier of either the disease or the part of the body affected, one could automatically construct a treatment to counteract this influence, simply by understanding the sympathies and antipathies of the planets. Astrological understanding of flora and fauna also allowed astrological medical practitioners to have easy access to a form of natural talismanic magic – whereby the planetary influence of herbs could be used to affect patients needing equilibrium to be re-established. Astrologer-physician Joseph Blagrave (1610-c. 1682) utilised the talismanic nature of some herbal remedies, prescribing his 'patients to wear a select number

---

289   MS Ashm 1501, art. 5, ff. 5-6v; cited in MacDonald, *Mystical Bedlam*, p. 29. MacDonald notes 'Napier's views about the importance of accurate information regarding his patients' symptoms are also illustrated by Ashml 1730, ff. 202, 205, and Ashml 232, f. 298.'

290   Culpeper, *English Physician*, 'To the Reader', sig *a2'-a2v.

of... herbs' gathered at astrologically appropriate times.[291] These were practical benefits of the astrological exploration of the essential natural magical identity and properties of the environment. It was a living system employing a unifying universal scope of meaning to select natural resources to steer the course of a sickness towards recovery – that is, to affect practical results through application of knowledge, understanding and informed action.

Artificial talismans such as astrological sigils, seals and images were also used in medical treatment. Talismans could draw forth elemental forces to return equilibrium to imbalanced humours. Precisely because elemental Fire and Water are considered to have opposite qualities (hot-and-dry and cold-and-moist respectively), Agrippa describes how images of 'Cancer, Scorpio and Pisces, because they do constitute the watery... triplicity, do prevail against hot and dry fevers'.[292] The scope of potential talismanic treatments was not limited to humoural readjustment – planetary and zodiacal symbolism was also utilised. The seal of Scorpio, made "correctly",[293] exercised dominion over scorpions and, by extension, all venomous things – it was therefore 'a most excellent Remedy against all Poyson and Diseases thereby infected.'[294] Astrological amulets were also prescribed to those suffering from a variety of mental and emotional disturbances.[295]

Even treatments not themselves especially astrological were carefully timed by election. Indeed, 'virtually all

---

291   Joseph Blagrave, *Astrological Practice of Physick* (London, 1671), p. 156.

292   Agrippa, *Three Books*, p. 375.

293   i.e. observing planetary hours.

294   *Supreme Mysteries of Nature*, p. 147.

295   See section on mind, body, and soul, Chapter 4.

physicians of the period employed astrology in their practice to determine appropriate days for bloodletting and purging and to set a schedule for administering medications.'[296] In a 'small Treatise' detailing a cure for smallpox which does not appear to have any explicit astrological dimension, the author adds an (expressly astrological) appendix on the basis that, after this work had been submitted 'in order to be Printed; it came into my Mind that I had given directions to *Vomit* such Persons as should be infected with the *Small Pox*... but had given no Instruction to the ignorant Tenders how to govern the Patient during the time that it is Working' and that 'therefore I will first shew (to such as have a little insight into *Astrology*) how to Elect a proper time for the Administration of the Medicine'.[297] So established was such a practice, even in 1685, that the author Lamport[298] added a whole appendix dedicated to including this vital astrological feature of treatment. Such was the perceived power of the natural magic of an astrological universe – bad timing might literally kill you. This kind of medical election presented the treatment in a universal context, and made both practitioner and patient uniquely aware of the environmental factors influencing their activity. Not only the disease and diagnosis, but the cure itself, became part of an unfolding destiny, interconnected through applied analysis of specific points in time and empowered by the influences of the stars. Using election, 'the medical astrologer could thus manipulate the forces of nature to heal his patients.'[299]

---

296   Traister, p. 104.

297   John Lamport, *A direct method of curing smallpox* (London, 1685), p. 17.

298   'alias Lampard'. Ibid, frontispiece.

299   MacDonald, *Mystical Bedlam*, p. 175.

MIND, BODY AND SOUL

Amongst the complaints, maladies and diseases treated by astrological medical practitioners were a whole subset of disorders affecting the patient's mind as well as body. Consideration of seventeenth-century attitudes to 'impairment of a principal internal mental faculty'[300] requires a careful approach. Comparisons between modern ideas of mind, body and their early modern considerations are, to say the least, problematic – 'early modern Europeans deployed a nosology that, over time, has became largely alien.'[301] Nevertheless, "psychiatry" is not in itself an anachronistic label for early modern treatment of madness.[302] There is compelling evidence that 'clergymen, astrologers, and magicians of all kinds treated mental disorders.'[303] Mental disorders were often explained, like physical maladies, by reference to the waxing and waning of astrological influence upon the victim's humoural temperament. However, we must remember that, within early modern psychiatry, 'the prevailing system of Galenic medicine still subordinated the body to the soul and medical authors usually passed decorously over the problematic mind-body relationship',[304] precisely because, for contemporaries, mind and body were two expressions of a

---

300 Gowland, 'The Problem of Early Modern Melancholy', p. 13.

301 Lederer, p. 147.

302 'psychology is certainly no more anachronistic a historical tool than, say, sociology. In fact, psychology was an innovation of the sixteenth century.' Lederer, p.21.

303 MacDonald, *Mystical Bedlam*, p. 176.

304 Lederer, p. 8. Lederer contextualises this statement by saying that 'our modern preoccupation with the mind/body "problem" was, for contemporaries, less problematic and based on a complex structural relationship between God, humans and the physical universe.' p. 147.

complex of underlying interrelations which included religious notions of the soul, free will and sin as much as ideas that might be considered analogous to modern epistemological categorisations of biology and psychology.

Astrology could also locate mental disorders in its (characteristically) total categorisation of human maladies. Mental and physical problems were described in a common astrological language, and were linked to the wider environment and motions of the universe. Just as physical complaints could be remedied by knowing the astrological sympathies and antipathies that would address the imbalance causing the illness, so too could diseases of the mind. The astrologer-physician Richard Napier's most (in)famous mental health case was the treatment of Viscount Purbeck, John Villiers (1591?-1658). Driven to apparent breakdown by the power-plays between his and his wife's ruthless aristocratic families, MacDonald assesses: 'Purbeck was almost certainly a manic depressive and alcoholic, and Napier treated his wild oscillations between 'merry madness' and deep melancholia with medicaments, management and amulets from 1622 to 1626 and then again in 1631-32.'[305]

Seventeenth-century astrology accepted an interlinked relation between mind and body, and because each could affect the other, a doctor would need to be sure he was treating the cause of the illness rather than merely a symptom. One of the first tasks of the astrologer-physician therefore was to determine whether the disease 'be in the minde, or in the body.' Culpeper offered astrological 'Aphorisms' for determining this ('the Sun, Moon and Ascendent rule the body, and their Lords the minde') followed by more detailed consideration – 'If Jupiter

---

305   MacDonald, 'Career of Astrological Medicine', p. 74-76.

be significator of the disease, it lies in the body, if it lies anywhere; for Jupiter never troubles the mind'.[306]

Precisely because early modern forms of psychiatry frequently interwove their understandings of mind, body and soul, astrology shared common ground with religious as well as occult discourses in treating infirmities of the mind. This can be observed most readily in the idea that 'sin corrupted the bodily humors physically.'[307] Transgression endangered the mind and body as well as the soul. Along with the corruption resulting from spiritual transgression, it was more widely understood that damage to, or degradation of, the physical body could itself impair mental faculties. This can be seen most obviously in early modern humoural understandings of the brain. In a compilation of medical treatises listed as 'being chiefly a Translation of the works' of French physician, Lazarus Riviere, we are told 'the greatest number of Diseases of the Head come from a Cold and Moist Distemper of the Brain', precisely because 'the Brain is that Mother of Moisture or Flegm, and Coldness long abiding draws moisture to itself.'[308] This kind of early modern assessment, and the resultant treatments to re-balance humours, should look fairly familiar to us by now.

As we have seen, seventeenth-century humours were still constructed from elementist premises, possessing elemental qualities that could be brought into balance using a variety of magical-medical means; many of which were, naturally, astrological. These could be applied to heal the unbalanced mind just as effectively as the dyscratic body. The cures offered for excess phlegm in the head were the

---

306   Culpeper, *Semeiotica Uranica*, pp. 106, 107.

307   Lederer, p. 18.

308   Lazarus Riverius, *The practice of physic in seventeen books* (London, 1668), p. 2.

same as other humoural treatments: 'Diet, Chirurgery and Physick', that is, (often expressly humoural) regulations of nutritive intake and procedures of bloodletting and purging supported by syrups, electuaries and other medicaments.[309] In addition to these, the types of treatments for the adjustment and regulation of humours we have already seen could be employed.

In addition to humoural and elementist comprehension of the brain, expressly astrological nosology – particularly the practice of *melothesia* (attributing parts of the body to the rulership of zodiacal signs) – was common in early modern neuroscience. Culpeper's *Semeiotica Uranica* offers us a typical early modern perspective on the sheer range of mental and physical brain (or, more commonly, simply 'head') maladies:

> 'Under Aries are... all diseases in the Head, as the Head-ach of all sorts, Vertigo, Frenzy, Lethargy, Forgetfulness, Catalepsie, Apoplexy, dead-Palsy, Coma, Falling-sickness, Convulsions, Cramps, Madness, Melancholy, Trembling.'[310]

We find here a whole range of cognitive, behavioural and pathological dysfunctions.

This association with Aries was by no means the only judgement on brain disease. According to Agrippa, citing such attributions to 'the doctrine of the Arabians', both the Sun and the Moon ruled the brain, while Mercury was associated with 'common sense'. [311] These planetary and zodiacal forces could be harnessed using the methods

---

309 Riverius, *The practice of physic in seventeen books*, p. 3-8.

310 Culpeper, *Semeiotica Uranica*, p. 89.

311 Agrippa, *Three Books*, p. 72.

already explored to treat a variety of kinds of impairment of neurological and psychological functions.

Early modern psychiatry also included astrologically-based humoural components to the experience and expression of what we modern thinkers might call emotional distress.[312] An imbalance of any of the humours would encourage perturbations that would make the subject's body and mind more susceptible to affect. This was the most basic early modern understanding of passions: they were affections because they were what affect us, they were perturbations treated as accidents that befall us – they were passions understood as what *moves* us. Some thinkers considered there to be inherently dangerous qualities in any impassioned or emotional state. So it is that theologian, poet and historian Nicolas Coeffeteau (1574-1623) presents the claim that 'as we call passions of the body diseases, wounds, paines, inflammations, incisions, and all other violent accidents which happen extraordinarily: so wee properly call passions of the soule, those infirmities wherewith she is afflicted and troubled...'[313] This kind of attitude culminated in the notion of *psychomachia*, the war for the soul in each of us between pious Christian rationality and base animalistic passions.

The pathologisation and demonization of the passions were not the only early modern comprehensions of emotionality. Other thinkers, in the tradition of the ancient philosophers Cicero, Plutarch and others, emphasised the passions as useful tools for ensuring proper moral conduct. Even the priest Thomas Wright (c.1561-1623),

---

312   'Through their sympathetic attraction (or antipathy) to other people, objects or celestial bodies, the four corruptible elements of the body caused motions or emotions in the soul.' Lederer, p. 25.

313   Nicolas Coeffeteau, *A Table of Humane Passions* (London, 1621), p. 18-19

who on the whole advocated a fairly "pro-psychomachia" position, declared that 'Passions are not onely, not wholy to be extinguished (as the Stoicks seemed to affirme) but sometimes to be moved, and *stirred vp for the service of virtue...*'[314] For example, 'shamefastnesse brideleth vs of many loose affections, which would otherwise bee ranging abroad.'[315] Rather than advocating a total repression of all impassioned states in favour of some kind of unadulterated rationality, one passion could be used to regulate – or, as in the example of shame, restrain – another.[316]

To return to a theological angle, the passions were thought to originate in the sensitive faculties of the Aristotelian tripartite soul – the part shared with animals – and were considered in essence the movement of the soul towards stimuli it deemed good, beneficial or pleasurable and away from those perceived as bad, detrimental or painful. As such, they were ordained by God as part of our immortal souls: their actions and malfunctions fell as much under the purview of the priest as the physician.

Beyond emotional pathology, the vast, intricate breadth and wealth of passionate human experience was comprehended with humoural elementist understandings. Anger was considered a Fiery choleric passion; lust and joy were both Airy sanguine affections; grief, a condition associated particularly with the Watery phlegmatic temper; sorrow, a product of the Earthy black bile, melancholy. This last example is probably the clearest of a humour and an

---

314 Thomas Wright, *The Passions of the Minde in Generall* (London, 1604), p. 17

315 Wright, *The Passions of the Minde*, p. 17

316 For more on psychomachia and the cultivation of the passions, see Christopher Tilmouth's excellent *Passion's Triumph Over Reason: A history of the moral imagination from Spenser to Rochester* (Oxford, 2007).

impassioned state sharing terminology, although there are also plenty of instances of 'Choler' referring both to humour and passion.[317] Exposure (a magical principle in itself) to Fiery things could encourage one to experience and express 'boldness', anger or any of the other Fiery passions.

The interaction of humours and passions was two-way. This interrelation was described by Wright in his popular *Passions of the Minde in Generall*, judging that 'Passions ingender Humors, and Humors breed Passions'.[318] So the heavens could affect our quality of experience and methods of expression, and our very physical and mental functioning, while habit and habituation of personality, behaviour, even diet, would encourage the cultivation of the humours – the bodily reflections of the cosmic building blocks of the elementist universe – that would continue these physiological-emotional feedback loops.

The interrelations between religiosity and the occult forces underpinning the universe were also by no means a "one-way system", and the multiplicity of Christian magical practices attest to this. Richard Napier was not only an astrologer-physician of considerable renown, but also a clergyman, who, in addition, practiced angelic magic – for expressly medical purposes. In 1619 he conjured the Archangel Raphael for a medical consult to help diagnose clients. A transcript of the conversation between doctor and angel revealed 'Raphael's opinion that five of Napier's patients were bewitched and predictions that two of them would recover.'[319] The biographer John Aubrey (1626-1697) and Lilly both attested that such conjurations were common, even the

---

317   See both Wright, *The Passions of the Minde* and Coeffeteau, *A Table of Humane Passions* passim.

318   Wright, *The Passions of the Minde*, p. 64

319   Ashml. 235, ff. 186v-92v; cited in MacDonald, *Mystical Bedlam*, p. 210.

norm, in Napier's practice – furthermore, they considered this to be testament not of his magical prowess conflicting with his religious position, but of Napier's great piety.[320]

As Don C. Skemer has pointed out, there was a medieval practice in which 'amuletic texts could also be inscribed on small metal sheets (*lamellae* or *laminae*) for medical use on the body...'[321] Not only did this continue into the early modern period, but these lamen could also be used for rectifying impairments of mental faculties. The 'amuletic texts' were frequently Biblical passages. The reciting of Biblical passages and Christian prayers were often treatments in themselves,[322] as well as being a frequent part of the administering of healing amulets.[323] Such administrations would frequently use astrological timing. In Sloane MS 3851, the grimoire of London cunning-man Arthur Gauntlet, there are instructions for engraving magical symbols onto a cooking pot in which to wash 'weakened things': the engraving was to be done in the hour of the Sun and Psalm 7:2 was to be read over the water seven times.[324] Significantly, these instructions are contained in a section of the grimoire entitled 'Magnus Medicus est Naturae Minister' ('The Great Doctor is the Servant of Nature'): editor David Rankine notes that the "great doctor" was a common way to refer to Christ himself as a physician.[325]

---

320 MacDonald, *Mystical Bedlam*, pp. 18, 16.

321 Don C. Skemer, *Binding Words: Textual Amulets in the Middle Ages* (Pennsylvania, 2006), p. 13.

322 See Davies, *Popular Magic*, p. 147-8.

323 For example, Richard Napier's magical amulet for Sir Thomas Myddleton. MacDonald, 'Career', p. 73-4; also MacDonald, *Mystical Bedlam*, p. 213-14.

324 *The Grimoire of Arthur Gauntlet*, ed. by David Rankine (London, 2011), p. 264.

325 *The Grimoire of Arthur Gauntlet*, p. 264 n 349.

We see in such Psalm charms various rituals of medication, often designed to be self-administered. Such charms therefore extended the act of treating ailments out of the consultation room of cunning-folk and into the everyday lives of their patient-clients. As employed in construction and consecration of magical objects such as these medical tools, they were a magical means to activate, as well as recharge, one's medicine with intent and language recognisable as pious and effective. Indeed, in considering the relations between magic and Christianity we should bear in mind the claim of Walter Raleigh (1554-1618), that 'the art of magic is the art of worshipping God'.[326] Magic and religion were especially co-mingled in the practice of astrology, and most overtly in the practices of astrologers such as Dee, Napier, Forman and even Lilly.[327]

By astrological assessment, the mind, like any other phenomenon of the universe, existed in a context of forces that influenced all life, time and events. Understandably then, 'the astrologer and his clients were seldom content to list a single factor as the sole cause of a case of mental disorder.'[328] Astrology was used to analyse and understand an illness – whether of the body or mind – not merely to find

---

326   K.M. Briggs, *Pale Hecate's Team* (London, 1962), p. 44. The same sentiment found in Agrippa, *Fourth Book*, sig A2v.

327   There is myriad study of Dr Dee's "pious magic", but for his astrology specifically, see Geörgi Szőnyi, *John Dee's Occultism* (New York, 2004), p. 157-61; for Napier, see MacDonald, *Mystical Bedlam*, (especially p. 18) for details of a direct line of astrological-magical transmission between himself and Dee; for Forman see Lauren Kassell, *Medicine and Magic in Elizabethan London: Simon Forman – Astrologer, Alchemist, and Physician* (Oxford, 2005); for Lilly, see Capp, *Astrology*, p. 54 and Thomas p. 230, 632. While Lilly eventually turned his back on other magical practices, Curry asserts that 'his astrology never lost its divinatory, implicitly magical quality.' Curry, p. 31

328   MacDonald, *Mystical Bedlam*, p. 173.

causes. Astrologers used their figures as warning systems for times when the stars might predispose the humoural temperaments of their clients to certain mental afflictions, not to categorically blame one particular astrological configuration. Astrology outlined all kinds of phenomena as contributing to impairment of mental faculties. Indeed, 'most people in early seventeenth-century England saw no theoretical incompatibility among the different kinds of explanation for mental disorders, and many practitioners combined therapies justified by medical, magical, and religious beliefs'.[329]

Such therapies took full advantage of the manipulation of influences facilitated by astrological understanding. The patient's mind would "soak up" what it was exposed to, so the correct management of environmental stimulus could be vital for recovery. The doctrine of the "six non-natural things" – 'diet, retention and evacuation, air [crucially, sometimes referred to as 'the heavens' i.e. the stars], exercise, sleeping and waking, and the passions' was utilised to properly affect this management of the humours.[330] This management of environmental stimuli could be relatively mundane – 'Forman sometimes prescribed a change in diet or behaviour (regimen) rather than any specific medical intervention', such as the standard purges and blood-letting most common in early modern medical treatments.[331] He would often judge that patients suffering from melancholy 'must haue comfortable things and be merry and give

329   Ibid, p. 177.

330   Ibid, p. 195; citing Robert Burton, *Anatomy of Melancholy* (Oxford, 1621), p. 217, and Kocher, *Science and Religion in Elizabethan England* (San Marino, 1953), p. 292-3.

331   Traister, p. 71.

her sweete & comfortable meat.'[332] This was not merely comfort-eating for the depressed. The inherent occult properties of these foods and activities would have an effect on the patient's humours – their magical physiology. Such 'comfortable things' were astrologically justified treatments with rational reasoning derived from magical premises of humoural theory, contagion and exposure.

Astrological interrelation meant all things transmitted an effect as well as receiving one. A diseased mind, and in particular a diseased 'Imagination', not only absorbed but transmitted an influence that would affect a change in humours and exert a negative influence on the bodies and minds of people around them.[333] What might nowadays be explained as the "power of suggestion" was understood as effects of an underlying link between knowledge and the physical body. The physician John Cotta (c. 1575-1627/8), a staunch critic of astrology, popularised the cases of two female patients who, following being misdiagnosed, promptly developed the very diseases they had been told they had already contracted.[334] Richard Napier noted the case of Joan Neighbor, who became melancholic after merely hearing about a suicide.[335] Knowledge itself could cause mental and physical ailments by interacting with an individual's consciousness. Thus early modern psychology writer Robert Burton (1577-1640) describes the 'Imagination' as 'the *medium deferens* of passions' which themselves acted upon one's character as one's 'humours

---

332   MS Ash. 226: 136r; cited in Traister, p. 71.

333   MacDonald, *Mystical Bedlam*, p. 182.

334   John Cotta, *A Short Discouerie of severall sorts of ignorant and unconsiderate Practitioners of Physicke in England*, (London, 1619), p. 51-3.

335   Neighbor's case in Asml. 230, f. 162; cited in MacDonald, *Mystical Bedlam*, p. 182.

disposed'.[336] Astrology was an essential tool in discerning the influences that an unwary person's imagination could catch and be manipulated by. Moreover, it could prescribe treatments for these plagued individuals.

Lilly writes of an astrological sigil made for his master Gilbert Wright (d. 1627) by Simon Forman to prevent Wright being haunted by the spirit of a man who had killed himself in a room in which Wright had stayed. This spirit was now provoking Wright himself to suicide.[337] This presents us with a slightly different early modern modelling of the apparently contagious nature of mental disorders; one where Wright's suicidal tendencies were still picked up by geographical proximity but now anthropomorphised into the form of a malevolent ghostly tempter, or 'revenant'.[338] Such a diagnosis of malevolent spiritual agency was remarkable but far from unusual.[339] Wright apparently wore his protective sigil 'continually until he died,' and, thankfully, 'was never more molested by the spirit'.[340] We might see in Wright's sigil of protection from spirits an astrological-magical anxiolytic treatment. It has been calculated that out of all Richard Napier's consultations which included mention of amulets, 20.3% were for those 'tempted to suicide'.[341] Forman also dealt with cases of haunted melancholic people tempted to

---

336 Burton, Anatomy of Melancholy, p. 127-8.

337 Lilly, *History of his Life and Times* (London, 1822), p. 33-4. This magical item is included in Lilly's description of several of the sigils that were in Margaret Wright's possession when she died; 'some of Jupiter in Trine, others of the nature of Venus, some of iron, and one of gold'. Lilly, *History of his Life and Times* (London, 1822), p. 32.

338 Lederer, p. 244.

339 MacDonald and Murphy, *Sleepless Souls*, p. 43.

340 Lilly, *History of his Life and Times* (London, 1822), p. 33-4.

341 MacDonald, *Mystical Bedlam*, p. 294 n. 198, 182.

self-harm and suicide by evil spirits – he managed to help one Susan Cuckston 'to handle pins and knives without inflicting self-harm' using a purge treatment.[342]

We can feasibly conjecture about early modern conceptions of positive effects of astrological amulets based upon an early modern conception of the power of suggestion, particularly when we take into account that during this period it had been 'asserted that people who were terrified by the plague were more vulnerable to the disease.'[343] Similarly, Forman discusses how poor mental health could impair the body's ability to fight off disease: a disrupted mind would influence the body to 'languish long in a small disease'.[344] Robert Burton highlights how humoural theory (which astrology incorporated as part of its universal system of meaning) could be itself a way to understand the laws of magic. Magical and astrological medicine 'doth more strange cures th[a]n [those of a] rationall Physition... because the patient puts his confidence in him... Tis opinion alone, saith Cardan, that makes or marres Physitions'.[345] It is in this context we should understand Forman's insistence upon earning the trust of his patients. Astrology could make the most accurate medical diagnoses, 'thereby winning the confidence of the patient'[346] and therefore ensuring that the treatment would be well received by the patient's body and mind. The activity of proscribing was itself bolstered by the authority that astrological knowledge

---

342 Kassell, *Medicine and Magic*, p. 150; citing Ashm. 355, p. 127-30.

343 MacDonald, *Mystical Bedlam*, p. 182; citing Richard Hunter and Ida Macalpine, comps., *Three Hundred Years of Psychiatry*, 1535-1860 (London, 1963), p. 111.

344 Ashm. 343, fo. 138v; cited in Kassell, *Medicine and Magic*, p. 169.

345 Burton, *Anatomy of Melancholy*, p. 127.

346 Kassell, *Medicine and Magic*, p. 148.

bestowed upon the medical practitioner. Forman noted that 'the verie presence of the physician aswel as the medison shall be verie comfortable to the sick and the sick shall rejoice in and have in great regard the phisisione and he shall doe the sicke more good.'[347] Astrological practice was not merely a matter of knowing what was wrong, or even how to remedy it – it was a conscientious administering activity that required the astrologer to enter into a relationship with their clients and earn their trust.

Individual instances of psychological problems were astrologically considered as part of the wider universe, and considered in the same language. Just as astrology reconciled the apparent difference of celestial and terrestrial phenomena into a cohesive spectrum of reflecting scales so the mental and the physical were considered within a unifying analytical framework. Astrology mapped the multiplicity of environmental factors for imbalance and impairment of mental faculties. Astrologers analysed individuals and offered treatment for mental disorders within a context of influences that combined physiology, religion and magic. Astrological utility and elaboration of humoural theory explored the microcosm of a patient's mind using the macrocosm of the stars. Environmental influences were managed to create a healing regimen, but the field-like nature of 'Imagination' meant it also interacted with the world as it was influenced. The idea of a diseased mind being somehow contagious demonstrates the crucial principle that knowledge has a tangible and magical effect on the knower. Existing in this magical universe meant both affecting and being affected by it, and understanding itself could alter and manipulate this two-way process of effect.

---

347   Ashm. 1495, fo. 477v; cited in Kassell, *Medicine and Magic*, p. 150.

Personal Consultancy

The final forms of personal astrology to be discussed are the varied and various non-medical personal consultations that practitioners of astrology gave. Local practitioners were also often asked to help bring something about – to bless or otherwise enchant or protect. Astrology offered knowledge and practice of a 'rich variety of magical... practices to deal with everyday frustrations, longings and dilemmas'.[348]

Much of an astrological practitioner's workload came in the form of providing information and understanding. The most common question put to an astrological practitioner was *'quid agendum'*: 'what's to be done'.[349] Astrology's universal comprehensiveness allowed it to answer questions concerning anything. Offered the chance to know about anything, most early modern people were interested in their relationships. Love consults were not limited to forecasts of spouse material, though these were common.[350] They included relationship advice and marriage counselling. This could even extend to magical action – cunning-folk sometimes offered to make 'ill husbands to be good to their wifes'.[351] Astrology considered the love-lives and kinships of individuals as part of the overall pattern of the universe. Likewise, complicated family matters could be consoled and explained, indeed 'every kind of domestic entanglement was ventilated in the astrologer's consulting-room.'[352] In

---

348 Martin Ingram, 'From Reformation to Toleration: Popular Religious Cultures in England, 1540-1690', in Tim Harris (ed.), *Popular Culture in England*, c. 1500-1850 (London, 1995), p. 108.

349 Thomas, p. 314-15.

350 See Thomas, p. 373-4.

351 Cited in Davies, *Popular Magic*, p. 101.

352 Thomas, p. 374-5.

particular, astrology provided the paternity tests of its day for uncertain men and women, demonstrating a performativity of astrological announcements about personal identity.[353] In an era of aristocratic bloodlines, astrological knowledge about your parentage could literally change your life.

Astrological practitioners generated spontaneous information through knowledge-at-a-distance divination. Horary techniques, the 'openly divinatory kind of astrology',[354] proved essential for this practice. Ritualisation of consultation provided a time-point focus to astrologically locate and analyse profundity. The extent to which local horary activity was ritualised can be seen in the case of John Vaux, a curate, astrologer and cunning-man, who would often draw up his astrological figures and calculations on the communion altar – doubtlessly with the purpose of ensuring that casting and interpretation were guided by God.[355] Piety was an indication of a great astrologer and magician as well as a priest.

The other main area of astrological divination was detection magic. Astrology offered advice for treasure-seeking[356] and was also 'one of the most common techniques employed for finding lost property'.[357] This could also include stolen property – in a letter dated 28th July 1650 astrologer Vincent Wing (1619-1668) asked Lilly to help interpret

---

353   Ashm. 390, ff. 161-5, Ashm. 182, f. 86, Ashm. 427, f. 201v; cited in Thomas, p. 374.

354   Curry, p. 30.

355   Davies, *Popular Magic*, p. 78.

356   Forman, Lilly, Napier, Culpeper, Gadbury 'and others' all hunted for treasure using astrology – Thomas, p. 377; Davies, *Popular Magic* pp. 93-95.

357   Davies, *Popular Magic*, p. 100.

a figure to find stolen linen for an MP's wife.[358] Similarly, detection magic could be used to find people, as evidenced by Booker's note to Lilly asking him to locate Booker's absconded son Samuel.[359] As with horary work, ritual was important, perhaps even essential, in detection magic. One magical practitioner in 1631 claimed 'any man going about to find out stolen goods doth it with great difficulty, with fasting and praying three days together and great pains taken therein.'[360] Like the worried parents of sick children who seemed to want only a prognosis, some merely wished to know if they would ever get their belongings back. However, astrological practitioners also used their knowledge to influence the return of stolen goods.[361] Astrology offered both closure and an avenue of hope for the practitioner and client to explore together.

Since astrology could find both people and stolen goods, it could also locate and identify thieves. Many practitioners offered to magically compel the thief to return the property. There were many different techniques of anti-thief magic – as well as horary figures to identify offenders, 'written charms were also used to afflict thieves and thereby force them into returning goods, and spirits could also be conjured up to do likewise.'[362] There are examples of astrological images that could be cast to find criminals or ward off thieves, such as the image of the third face of Cancer and that of the seventeenth mansion of the Moon.[363] The fear of magical

---

358   MS Ash. 423 II, 174; cited in Curry, p. 33.

359   MS Ash. 180, f. 122; cited in Capp, Astrology, p. 56.

360   Cited in Thomas, p. 255.

361   Davies, *Popular Magic*, p. 96-101.

362   Ibid, p. 101.

363   Agrippa, *Three Books*, p. 377; Agrippa, *Three Books*, p. 393.

reprisal itself was also hoped to induce enough of an effect to achieve a speedy recovery.[364] The social justice implications of this are worth considering – 'astrology could be a useful deterrent'[365] in any number of areas. In fact for every field of divination, astrology provided the techniques, understanding and agency to affect the subject of the divination, whether by specific timing, identifying unknown parties or by using astrological knowledge to affect magical results.

A hand-written home protection prayer-charm from the end of seventeenth-century to 'bequeath thys place all about and all my goods within and without to the Blessed trinity that one god... [to allow] no thee[v]es feet goe' concludes with charging the planets and the twelve signs to keep the house safe, each astrological glyph written in their magical sequences.[366] The totality of the planetary and zodiacal governances could be employed to protect against every eventuality. A manageable astrological taxonomy of the complete mechanics of the universe allowed one to invoke and charge these forces with tasks and functions. This was the function of symbolising cosmic forces with glyphs – the extensive corresponding powers, responsibilities and influences of the planets and signs could be symbolised in their summarising glyphs. Hence 'there was also considerable use of overtly magical words and phrases, spirit names, occult symbols, planetary signs, and astrological terms' in the various magical charms offered by astrological practitioners.[367]

---

364 'The deterrent effect of their reputations was, in fact, the most important asset cunning-folk had in this respect.' Davies, *Popular Magic*, p. 97.

365 Thomas, p. 410.

366 MS Cod. Gaster, No. 1592); cited in M. Gaster, 'English Charms of the Seventeenth Century', *Folklore*, 21, no 3 (Sep, 1910), p. 375-78.

367 Davies, *Popular Magic*, p. 148.

Astrological symbolism played an important interpretive role in other forms of magic – most of which were practiced by astrologers. Geomantic divination, despite its late arrival into English vernacular, was very popular with magical practitioners.[368] Forman, Napier and the occultist Robert Fludd (bap. 1574, d. 1637) even 'formed a sort of succession especially in astrological and geomantic studies.'[369] Likewise, Davies judges that village cunning-folk who practised astrology 'would certainly appreciate the detailed practical guide to astromantic and geomantic divination, and the diagrams showing the various signs and characters of the planets and their angels' in John Heydon's *Theomagia*.[370] Astrological symbolism underlay geomancy – Cattan stated that geomancy 'doth participate with Astrologie, and is called her daughter.'[371] The sixteen "answers" or characters that made up the geomantic system had expressly astrological correspondences – the figure *Carcer* (Prison) for example, with a divinatory meaning of 'ill in all things', is attributed by Cattan to dark Scorpio.[372] Each of the sixteen figures had an astrological identity, although the specific attributions of the figures to the zodiacal signs varied slightly from handbook to handbook.[373] However, astrological symbolism

---

368 *The Geomancie of Mr Christopher Cattan*, was only transcribed into English in 1591, but proved so popular it required a reprint in 1608. See Skinner, p. 128.

369 Skinner, *Terrestrial Astrology*, p. 131; citing J.B. Craven, *Doctor Robert Fludd* (London, 1902).

370 Davies, *Popular Magic*, p. 124.

371 Cited in Skinner, p. 129.

372 Christopher Cattan, *Geomancie* (London, 1591), p. 56.

373 So, to continue the example, although Cattan ascribes Scorpio to Carcer, the *Fourth Book of Occult Philosophy* identifies Carcer as associated with Capricorn, while Agrippa's second of the second of

also worked at a more fundamental level in the geomantic divination process. A full geomantic cast would consist of generating twelve initial figures followed by three final figures which would be interpreted to provide a general answer to the inquiry.[374] The initial twelve were assigned in their order of appearance to the astrological diagram that represented the twelve houses of the heavens, in order to locate information more directly related to the question at hand.[375] This was a use of an astrological taxonomy (the house system and its twelve-part categorisation of human life), not to astronomically map celestial bodies, but to plot randomly generated figures into a magical sequence to derive particular significances for divining answers. The position of a geomantic figure in a particular house described the area of life that this figure affected, and the zodiac attributes of the figures were used to further interpret the figure's significance. Astrological symbolism aided the practice of geomancy by providing additional symbolic correspondences, links and interpretations: 'as far as geomancy is concerned, astrology is an interpretive system.'[376] Astrological knowledge added a powerful advantage to the user of geomantic magic. John Heydon even declared 'That No Divination without Astromancy and Geomancy is perfect.'[377]

---

the *Three Books of Occult Philosophy* calls it the figure of Pisces. See the Appendix 1 in Skinner, *Terrestrial Astrology*, p. 233.

374   Cattan, p. 3-11; Heydon, *Theomagia*, p. 1-10.

375   Cattan, p. 59-66; Heydon, *Theomagia*, p. 66. Large sections were given over in both works to what each figure meant in each house – Ibid, ii, p. 1-165.

376   Skinner, p. 204.

377   Heydon, *Theomagia*, p. 243. This is itself an alteration and extension of a chapter title in Agrippa's *Three Books* which states that 'no divination without astrology is perfect.' Agrippa, *Three Books*, Book II, Chapter LIII.

Astrological practitioners were not merely occult polymaths interested in various disconnected magical practices. Astrological structure, symbolism, theory and practice all contributed to, and even underlay, a deeper understanding, and therefore use of, other magical systems. This cross-pollination of astrology and other magic systems has been described as a 'blurring of different magical beliefs... characteristic of the period.'[378] I agree that these beliefs and systems co-mingled in a particularly striking way in the seventeenth century, but would certainly consider this magical syncretisation of apparently discrete beliefs and practices to be more than mere 'blurring'. Astrological practitioners combined their magical studies into wider cohesive universal systems, to explore occult influence in every aspect of existence. Forman expresses how astrology was the foundation of all study –

'for astrologie is the booke and course of all naturalle things, the grounds of physicke and mother of all artes what so ever. And without that thou canst doe nothing in phisicke nor magick.'[379]

The glaring overlaps in the theories and practices of astrologers, cunning-folk who used astrology, and ceremonial magicians, make distinguishing between these roles difficult. However this difficulty does not arise from interrelations of magical systems being hazily or indistinctly lumped together, but rather from the organic manner in which they associated and supported the practices of each other. The sheer utility of combining symbolism of different magical activities, reconciling supportive theories, principles and techniques

---

378   Thomas, p. 758.

379   MS. Ashm. 355: 48v; cited in Traister, p. 99.

into a complete practice, allowed magical practitioners of all kinds to better understand and therefore act in the magical universe. Astrology was a magical system of knowledge and activity that fed into and expanded the correspondences and interrelations of other magical systems and their interactions with this magical universe. It is for this reason that, when it came to astrologers and astrological practitioners, 'in practice many of these were indistinguishable from the village wizards.'[380]

SOCIAL CONCLUSIONS

Astrology was a vital interpretive craft for analysis of magic itself as well as for the large-scale movements of the universe, political developments and individuals and their groupings. Its symbolism fundamentally contributed to the theoretical knowledge and practical activity of other magical systems. Astrological practitioners dealt in all sorts of magic. Geomancy is a significant example, as this practice was not based upon an empirical map of celestial influence at a particular point in time (as in horary work), but on an arbitrary sequencing of stylised but randomly-generated data. Its practice required a belief in an underlying life or intellect to the universe itself that would communicate through certain "random" (or rather, magical) acts – say, by ensuring mathematically generated geomantic figures did indeed answer a question. This organic universe is an expressly magical model. One of the most ardent proponents of geomancy was Fludd, who 'saw the universe animated by a living soul and ruled by spiritual essences, angelic powers

---

380   Thomas, p. 358.

and a whole machinery of planetary intelligences.'[381] As has been observed, 'in the post-Restoration world, seen through the window of contemporary astrology, a line was drawn – not between magic and reason, as is so often assumed, but through magic, dividing it into acceptable and unacceptable sorts.'[382] Including principles such as contagion and sympathy, we find the foundations (and many practices) of astrology were deeply magical. In the motions of the stars, the universe narrated its story, relating itself to itself in an ongoing interrelation. It is this active engagement with a magical universe, of being part of the expressions of cosmos, that made astrology a spiritual as well as practical craft. It united the individual with existence, finding a role for one as an active participant in a magical universe. This is the context of the manner in which seventeenth-century English astrology operated as a practical Christian theology – as a parallel to the Church rather than competitor. Astrologers' practices were certainly different, but their roles as intermediaries, interpreters and even liminaries between the divine and the everyday were not.

The ritualised ceremonies of astrological consults, that provided both information and treatment, further facilitated the significances of interpretative astrological techniques. Technical readings of positions and relations of the stars were only one dimension of a consultation – astrological techniques were supported by the setting in which the consult took place. Ritualisation of the consulting process highlights the necessity of the authority and liminality of the astrological practitioner as an interpreter of existence's magical undercurrents. The practitioner united querent and question in their answers by being the intercessor between

---

381   Skinner, p. 132.

382   Curry, p. 39.

the two. It is in this context we should understand certain popular anxiety about Forman entering the names of his clients alongside the figures he would cast for them.[383] This was not solely a fear of 'diabolic overtones' in the contract-like nature of this practice. Names were not just signifiers; they were a powerful magical handle that contained an essence or attachment to what they signified. This was a basis of the use of angelic names in conjuration, as well as the carving of planetary glyphs into talismans. An individual and their situation were unified and explored in a single magical act.

This unification of individual and situation was focused around the point at which astrological knowledge informed the client. Held within the moment at which a question was asked was an encoded answer. Horary astrology decoded patterns and inertias within these particular moments. This understanding was itself a collaboration between astrological practitioner and querent, and encouraged further action in light of fuller awareness. The manner in which this expanded awareness supported action is demonstrated in the way astrology located medical consultation 'in a fruitful context for the patient by providing the symbolic, interpretive, therapeutic, and social dimensions necessary for the completion of a successful healing act.'[384] We have already seen that astrological practitioners offered to magically affect the subjects they explained. This search for knowledge, and its expansion into the manipulation of effect, illustrates the implicit agency that astrology offered – to engineer and manage as well as explain favourable outcomes.

---

383   Kassell, *Medicine and Magic*, p. 170.

384   Ronald Sawyer, 'Patients, Healers and Disease in the Southeast Midlands, 1597-1634', Ph.D. thesis, University of Wisconsin, 1986, p. 293; cited in Kassell, *Medicine and Magic*, p. 128.

Astrological knowledge and action themselves required management. We have seen how mass societal phenomena were worked into cohesive social theory using astrologically-principled research. Likewise, personal services were improved by more accurate time- and note-keeping. Casenote review offered improvement and refinement of astrological diagnoses, to forecast, to offer advice and to otherwise affect the situation. Finally, this management extended to the manifestation of interpretation – that is, the behaviour and conduct of the interpreter. Issues concerning placebos, suggestion, deterrents, trust and authority reflect how the act of interpreting knowledge had significant effects – sometimes as much as the information or understanding itself.

Seventeenth-century English astrology treated certain knowledge as having a somewhat magical nature. A diseased and contagious imagination, and the influence upon this imagination by astrological conditions, could have tangible effect on the sanity and body of individuals and society in general. The very links between body and mind in early modern thinking reflect how knowledge could have effects through underlying magical principles. Even in divination, knowledge was encoded and hidden ("occult") in the stars, yet was always available to be summoned. Astrological knowledge made an intervention the instant it was called upon, which was based upon assessing the very point in time of that intervention. This assessment of astrology's own place in constructing information was based upon an inherent principle – that the universe was "narrating itself" across a time-span of ordained interrelation. There was no random time to make a horary question, there was destiny in all affairs, and knowledge itself was an active participant in this astrological story of fate. By understanding astrological-magical sympathies and antipathies, the underlying natures and operations of celestial forces, diagnosis *was* a treatment.

By knowing the astrological identity of the problem, one could automatically relate it to its relevant antidotes, and prescribe a way to manipulate the dilemma. It is for these reasons that 'astrology, though beginning as a system of explanation, thus ended as one which held out the prospect of control.'[385] The essence of the malady or general situation was considered within the same framework of interrelations as the essence of its resolution. The astrological practitioner truly did offer 'the prospect of that greater freedom which comes from self-knowledge.'[386] This knowledge was unified with action in the grand interlinking and reflecting scales of astrology.

Social astrology illustrates the most personally affecting connections of this grand unifying spectrum – those between individual, group, society and environment. It placed the ailments of particular parts of the human body within the same context as analysis of the body politic, and traced both of these back to fundamental principles of celestial influence. The combination of astrology and humoural theory also identified and analysed influences we would nowadays consider of a biological as well as psychological nature, likewise within the same fundamental framework. Such a combination reflects the interrelation of all existence, whether material or mental. Analysis of both mind and body were constructed from the same modelling assessments of a multiplicity of forces and contexts. This modelling assessment is the common unifying principle in all astrological activity. We *can* distinguish between different subject matters – the supposedly distinct "types" of astrology such as judicial, natural, etc. – but we must be aware that such categories are far from discrete. Such fields exist as overlapping areas of focus on a unified spectrum.

---

385   Thomas, p. 393.

386   Thomas, p. 391.

Astrology explored the magical identity of natural organisms through understanding their astrological properties and governorships. This brought together not only people, plants, trees, animals and other living things, but also non-living things ruled by or otherwise responsive to celestial forces. These included minerals, metals and other inorganic materials,[387] as well as abstract concepts, institutions and all the features of experiential life. Astrology considered that the human body itself 'is made of the same materials that the whole Universe is made of... namely of a composition of contrary Elements.'[388] All these things were considered to be containers of occult virtue – everything was communicating with and influencing everything else. Nothing and no-one was isolated. Human relation to the environment, to the universe in general and to the earth and our surroundings in particular, was not one of builder to materials, or of artist to media, but of a creation-wide dance or play of interrelation, in which the stars called the dance-steps as they moved. Environment was not simply something we acted upon or that acted upon us – such an attitude would have separated "man-made" and "natural" causes. All was an expression of the common unifying effect of the stars. The celestial influence that impacted upon humanity could have dangerous, even fatal results, yet this effect was felt throughout nature – the impact upon humanity and individuals was merely one expression of an overall process of effect. Astrology not only constructed or unveiled the social meaning of a personal tragedy, or even a particular kind of tragedy – it placed all tragedy and

---

387   Lilly's inclusion of 'Minerals' and 'Stones' fields in his cataloguing of the planets (Lilly, *Christian Astrology*, p. 57-82) is far from unusual for early modern English astrology.

388   Culpeper, *Semeiotica Uranica*, sig. A4.

victory in a unifying context that explored the complete
consequences that any phenomenon in an interconnected
magical universe would wreak. Astrology presented a
model with an infinite number of facets. It included social,
psychological and psychiatric subroutines to analyse all
other systems – it was an underlying magical system that
represented a grand unified set of principles, mechanics and
techniques for understanding and interacting with (and as
part of) an interrelated magical universe.

CHAPTER 5
CONCLUSIONS

ASTROLOGY WAS CERTAINLY A MAGICAL DISCIPLINE. Historians seeking to emphasise astrology's rationality have sought to distance astrology from magic. Such an emphasis is useful in approaching astrology on its own terms – yet this emphasis upon rationality should never come at the price of divorcing astrology from its magical roots and its clear use within magical activity. Geomancy's underlying astrological foundations have been briefly dealt with by Skinner, although mainly as part of the practices of the nineteenth-century occult revivalists, the Hermetic Order of the Golden Dawn. In terms of seventeenth-century study, Kassell and MacDonald have considered the diverse magical activities of individuals, providing useful beginnings for study into how astrological symbolism was utilised in general magical practices. Both Thomas and Capp note general usage of sigils and astrological magic, yet seem to consider it a peripheral activity to astrological divination. This book insists that the philosophy and utility of astrological images forms a central part of early modern astrology, and that this astrology informed a variety of other magical activities.

The totality of astrology's scope of analysis has been under-explored by historians. Thomas characterises astrology as having a universal 'comprehensiveness', and draws vital conclusions about the functions of astrology's universal breadth in 'bringing with it attempts at a universal natural law.'[389] This book provides further examination of the dynamic interrelations that astrology posited and explored within this comprehensive spectrum of meaning. Studies into the 'Great Chain of Being', a magical conception of a hierarchical universe, have looked at how existence is grouped and categorised into a chain of command but not at how the phenomena at each level actually relate to one another. Szőnyi has considered ways in which magicians have elevated themselves along this chain through exaltation, but has not considered how astrology could affect the world by directly manipulating its magical nature. My analysis of astrology and magic supports these investigations by more fully considering the astrological conception of the cosmos as an interrelation of surroundings, whether physical and immediate or celestial and abstract. My approach emphasises the universality and interconnectedness of early modern astrological conceptions of the "natural world" within a magical universe.

I have also placed the methods and manners by which astrological knowledge affected action at the forefront of the study of seventeenth-century astrology. Geneva, Rusche and Curry have addressed the political effects of astrology – Rusche and Geneva in specific terms of propaganda and cryptography, with Curry considering the broader political dimensions of astrology's role in early modern hegemony. MacDonald has begun discussion of knowledge's transformative value in his focus on early modern mental health, and Kassell has raised important issues of authority and trust in medical practice. However, this book emphasises ways in which astrological knowledge itself had performative and transformative functions in all areas of life – personal, societal, political and philosophical.

---

389 Thomas, p. 384.

Political and medical astrology offer us the clearest pictures of the importance of astrological interpretation, but these are just two examples of astrological understanding being itself knowledge-in-action.

SPECULATION

The study of astrology clearly has much to offer the history of magic. Applied broadly, study of early modern astrology can provide useful historical parallels for discussing the liminality of knowledge and status, and especially the functions of astrological practitioners as intermediaries, intercessors and interpreters. The religious dimensions of astrology, where the roles of astrologer and priest overlapped, have much to say about the status and utility of being an intermediary within communities and cultures, particularly of bridging the divine and the earthly. Likewise, expressly magical astrological practices provide many fascinating and useful examples of the functions of intercession, as well as of offering the means for direct action in a magical universe, endowing those with knowledge of and practice in astrological arts crucial roles within society. Study of astrology also makes essential contributions to the kind of epistemological approach being considered in Peek's studies of African divination systems[390] – in terms of assessing the analysis, interpretation and the construction of knowledge – as well as existentialist discussions of identity and responsibility.

---

390 Philip Peek (ed.), *African Divination Systems: Ways of Knowing* (Bloomington, 1991).

Summary

Early modern astrology provides us with a rich social and cultural focus for studying the fusing of magic and astrology, of knowledge and action, and of humans and their environment. As we have seen, astrology was based upon fundamentally magical premises and functioned in a variety of other magical practices. Study of astrology provides myriad examples of the illuminating, inspiring, and affecting nature of both illicit and orthodox forms of knowledge. It also presents early modern comprehension of knowledge itself as performative and magical, as well as showing how methods and models of understanding reflect or mimic the subjects being explored.

Astrology demonstrates how human understanding situates itself in relation to what it considers by exploring a universal and interrelating ontology of experience. I have tried to show not only how astrology presumes the interrelationship between individuals, nature and the cosmos, but how the art itself, reflecting that set of relationships, is conceived by its practitioners and audience as a dynamic, interrelated set of functions, interpretative devices and affective rituals. Seventeenth-century English astrology functioned as an early modern grand unified theory, as an interpretive and intercessory system for understanding and acting in a magical universe by constructing both correspondences and (what were conceived as) precise, functional significances from all phenomena.

BIBLIOGRAPHY

PRIMARY SOURCE

A collection of His Majesties gracious letters, speeches, messages and declarations since April 1660 (London, 1660).

Agrippa, H.C., *Fourth Book of Occult Philosophy*, translated by R. Turner (London, 1655).
Three Books of Occult Philosophy, translated by James Freake, ed. D. Tyson (St. Paul, 2004).

Ashmole, Elias, *Theatrum Chemicum Britannicum* (London, 1652).

Atwell, George, *An Apology, Or, Defense of the divine art of Natural Astrology* (London, 1660).

Blagrave, Joseph, *Astrological Practice of Physick* (London, 1671).

Booker, John, *The Bloody Almanack* (London, 1642).

Browne, Daniel, *A New Almanacke* (London, 1620).

Burton, Gregory, *Almanacke* (London, 1613).

Burton, Robert, *Anatomy of Melancholy* (Oxford, 1621).

Carpenter, Richard, *Astrology Proved Harmless, Useful, Pious* (London, 1656).

Cattan, Christopher, *Geomancie* (London, 1591).

Cockeram, Henry, *The English dictionarie* (London, 1626).

Coeffeteau, Nicolas, *A Table of Humane Passions* (London, 1621).

Cotta, John, *A Short Discouerie of severall sorts of ignorant and unconsiderate Practitioners of Physicke in England* (London, 1619).

Culpeper, Nicholas, *Semeiotica Uranica* (London, 1658).

Culpeper, Nicholas, *The English Physician* (London, 1652).

Dade, William, *Almanack* (London, 1647).

Edlyn, Richard, *Prae-nuncius sydereus* (London, 1664).

Fludd, Robert, *De supernaturali, naturali, paraenaturali et contranaturali microcosmi historia* (Oppenheim, 1619).

Gadbury, John, *The Doctrine of Nativities* (London, 1658). *The Nativity of the late King Charls* (London, 1659).

Gadbury, John (ed.), *The Works of George Wharton* (London, 1683).

Gell, Robert, *Stella Nova, A new starre leading wisemen unto Christ* (London, 1649).

Goad, John, *Astrometeorologica* (London, 1686).

Graunt, John, *Natural and Political Observations mentioned in a following Index, and made upon the Bills of Mortality* (London, 1662).

Heydon, Christopher, *An Astrological Discourse* (London, 1650).

Heydon, John, *Theomagia* (London, 1664).

Lamport, John, *A direct method of curing smallpox* (London, 1685).

Lilly, William, *A Prophecy of the White King and Dreadfull Dead-man Explaned* (London, 1644).
Anglicus (London, 1645).
Anglicus... for 1646 (London, 1645/6).
Christian Astrology (London, 1647).
History of his Life and Times (London, 1822 reprint).
Merlinin Anglici ephemeris (London, 1651).
Merlinus Anglicus Junior (London, 1644).

Monarchy or No Monarchy (London, 1651).
The Starry Messenger (London, 1645).

Martindale, Adam, *Country Almanack* (London, 1676).

On Bugbear Black Monday (1652).

Paracelsus Of the Supreme Mysteries of Nature, translated by R. Turner (London, 1656).

Partridge, Dorothy, *The woman's almanack, for the year 1694* (London, 1694).

Partridge, Seth, *Synopsis* (London, 1656).

Porta, Jean Baptiste, *Natural Magick* (London, 1658).

Riverius, Lazarus, *The practice of physic in seventeen books* (London, 1668).

The Grimoire of Arthur Gauntlet, ed. by David Rankine (London, 2011).

The Holy Bible (London, 1619).

Wharton, George, *An Astrologicall Judgement Upon His Majesties Martch* (Oxford, 1645).

Wharton, George, *Hemeroscopeion Anni aerae, 1653. Presenting the English and Roman Kalendar, Planetary Motions,Passions and Positions, Meteorologicall Observations, Chronologicall Collections, and Judgements Astrologicall, &c.* (London, 1653).

Wright, Thomas, *The Passions of the Minde in Generall* (London, 1604).

Secondary Source

Allen, D.C., *The Star-Crossed Renaissance* (London, 1966).

Briggs, K.M., *Pale Hecate's Team* (London, 1962).

Briggs, K.M., *The Last of the Astrologers* (London, 1974).

Burns, W.E., 'A Whig Apocalypse: Astrology, Millenarianism, and Politics in England During the Restoration Crisis, 1678-1683' in J.E. Force and R.H. Popkin (eds.), *Millenarianism and Messianism in Early Modern European Culture: The Millenarian Turn* (London, 2001).

Camden, Carroll, 'Elizabethan Astrological Medicine', *Annals of Medical History* 2 (1930), p. 217-26.

Capp, Bernard, *Astrology and the Popular Press: English Almanacs 1500-1800* (London, 1979).

Chapman, Allan, 'Astrological Medicine' in C. Webster (ed.), *Health, Medicine and Mortality in the Sixteenth Century* (Cambridge, 1979), p. 275-300.

Curry, Patrick, *Power and Prophecy* (Cambridge, 1989).

Davies, Owen, *Grimoires: A History of Magic Books* (Oxford, 2009)
Popular Magic (New York, 2007).

Dick, H.G., 'Students of Physic and Astrology', *Journal of the History of Medicine*, 1-2 (1946), p. 300-315 and 419-33.

Dobbs, B.J.T., 'Newton's Commentary on the Emerald Tablet of Hermes Trismegistus' in Ingrid Merkel & Allen G. Debus (eds.), *Hermeticism and the Renaissance* (Washington, 1988).

Gaster, M., 'English Charms of the Seventeenth Century', *Folklore*, 21, no 3 (Sep, 1910).

Geneva, Ann, *Astrology and the Seventeenth Century Mind* (Manchester, 1995).

Gowland, Angus, 'The Problem of Early Modern Melancholy', *Past & Present*, 191, (May, 2006), p. 77-120.

Hare, E.H., 'Medical Astrology and its Relation to Modern Psychiatry', *Proceedings of the Royal Society of Medicine*, 70, (February, 1977), p. 105-10.

Hart, Vaughan, *Art and Magic in the Court of the Stuarts* (London, 1994).

Henry, John, 'The Fragmentation of Renaissance Occultism and the Decline of Magic', *History of Science*, 46, I, 151 (March, 2008).

Hunter, Michael and Annabel Gregory (eds.), *An astrological diary of the seventeenth century : Samuel Jeake of Rye, 1652-1699* (Oxford, 1988).

Ingram, Martin, 'From Reformation to Toleration: Popular Religious Cultures in England, 1540-1690', in Tim Harris (ed.), *Popular Culture in England, c. 1500-1850* (London, 1995).

Josten, C.H. (ed.), *Elias Ashmole (1617-1692): his autobiographical and historical notes, his correspondence, and other contemporary sources relating to his life and work* (Oxford, 1966).

Kassell, Lauren, 'Food of Angels', in *Secrets of Nature* (London, 2001), p. 345-384.
Medicine and Magic in Elizabethan London: Simon Forman – Astrologer, Alchemist, and Physician (Oxford, 2005).

Lederer, David, *Madness, Religion and the State in Early Modern Europe* (Cambridge, 2006).

Lloyd, G.E.R., *Magic, Reason and Experience: Studies in the Origins and Development of Greek Science* (Cambridge, 1979).

MacDonald, Michael and T.R. Murphy, *Sleepless Souls* (Oxford, 1990).

MacDonald, Michael, 'The Career of Astrological Medicine in England' in O.P. Grell and A. Cunningham (eds.), *Religio Medici : Medicine and Religion in Seventeenth-century England* (Aldershot, 1996), p. 62-90.

MacDonald, Michael, *Mystical Bedlam: Madness, Anxiety and Healing in Seventeenth Century England* (Cambridge, 1981).

Middleton, John, 'Spirit Possession among the Lugbara', in J. Beattie and J. Middleton (eds.), *Spirit Mediumship and Society in Africa* (London, 1969).

Niccoli, Ottavia, *Prophecy and People in Renaissance Italy* (Princeton, 1990).

Peek, Philip, (ed.), *African Divination Systems: Ways of Knowing* (Bloomington, 1991).

Rachum, Ilan, 'The term 'Revolution' in Seventeenth-Century English Astrology', *History of European Ideas,* vol. 18, No. 6 (1994), p. 869-883.

Rusche, Harry, 'Merlini Anglici: Astrology and Propaganda from 1644 to 1651', *English Historical Review, 80* (1965), p. 322-333.
'Prophecies and Propaganda, 1641 to 1651', in *English Historical Review*, 84 (1969), p. 752-770.

Skemer, D.C., *Binding Words: Textual Amulets in the Middle Ages* (Pennsylvania, 2006).

Skinner, Stephen, *Terrestrial Astrology: Divination by Geomancy* (London, 1980).

Szőnyi, G.E., *'John Dee and Early Modern Occult Philosophy'*, Literature Compass 1 (2004), 1.

Szőnyi, G.E., *John Dee's Occultism* (New York, 2004).

Tester, S.J., *A History of Western Astrology* (Bury St. Edmunds, 1987).

Thomas, Keith, *Religion and the Decline of Magic* (London, 1991 reprint).

Tilmouth, Christopher, *Passion's Triumph over reason: a history of the moral imagination from Spenser to Rochester* (Oxford, 2007).

Traister, B.H., *The Notorious Astrological Physician of London: Works and Days of Simon Forman* (London, 2001).

Wojcik, J., 'Robert Boyle, The Conversion of the Jews, and Millenial Expectations', in J.E. Force and R.H. Popkin (eds.), *Millenarianism and Messianism in Early Modern European Culture: The Millenarian Turn* (Dordrecht, 2001).